Twayne's English Authors Series

Sylvia E. Bowman, *Editor*

INDIANA UNIVERSITY

Thomas Moore

TEAS 38

Thomas Moore

By MIRIAM ALLEN DeFORD

Twayne Publishers, Inc.   ::   New York

To

Agnes M. Miall

Friend and Fellow Writer—
Across the Atlantic and the Ocean of Years

Preface

Almost every biography of Thomas Moore begins with the statement that he was not a great poet, or indeed a great writer of any kind. That is quite true, although his contemporaries would not have agreed. He was unduly adulated and grossly overrated during his lifetime and for most of the half-century following his death. But another fact is also true: he has since been unduly and unjustly underrated and neglected. At least eight out of ten well-read young people today fail even to recognize his name (or they confuse him with Sir Thomas More)—though probably all their lives they have been hearing "The Last Rose of Summer" and "Believe Me, if All Those Endearing Young Charms." Two excellent biographies of Moore appeared nearly thirty years ago, but since then his name has seldom appeared in either books or articles in periodicals.

Yet Moore was an authentic if minor lyrical poet, a satirist of sometimes almost Swiftian stature, an outstanding biographer within the conventions of his time, a competent critic, and an accomplished and scholarly man of letters. Above all, he was one of the first, if not the very first, of the brilliant band of Irish writers who are ornaments of English literature; and although he spent most of his adult life in England, he was always thought of as the poetic voice of his native land.

The aim of this short volume is to reintroduce to a new generation of readers a writer unfairly forgotten, and to re-evaluate his standing in the light of contemporary criticism. Moore has been dead for more than a century, and the literary standards of his day are very far from those we entertain (and which may be equally ephemeral). We must judge him as a man of the late eighteenth and early nineteenth centuries; but we must also seek for what remains of permanent value in his work.

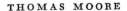

We shall consider first the world into which he was born and in which he grew up, the life he lived, and the circles in which he moved. Then we shall view him as a Romantic poet, a song-writer to whom the music was as important as the words to which it was set; as a translator and adaptor of light Classic verse in the tradition of the late eighteenth century, which was the period of his youth; as a social, political, and religious satirist in verse; as the author of lush and florid narrative poems; as a biographer and historian; as a serious (and pedantic) seeker after religious truths; and as a diarist. From all these considerations there should emerge a composite picture which will enable us to assess Moore's place in English literary history.

The problem in writing about Thomas Moore is not that of search but of selection. He himself was a far too voluminous writer, in verse at least, and too much was written about him by his contemporaries (just as too little has been written about him in recent years); and the various critical pronouncements are colored by the personal and political views of the critics. To an Irish patriot of his own time, Moore was one thing; to an English Whig, another; to an English Tory, still a third. He was the delight and darling of his friends; and he had no personal, though many political, enemies. What we must do is to go directly to his writing itself, and make our judgments on that basis alone with no extraneous considerations.

As Moore himself wrote in a letter to Samuel Rogers: "Biography is like dot engraving, made up of little minute points, which must all be attended to, or the effect is lost." So too is criticism. And when all the "little minute points" are put in their proper place, the portrait stands solidly before us on the page.

MIRIAM ALLEN DEFORD

Contents

Chronology

1779 Thomas Moore born May 28 in Dublin, Ireland; the first child of John and Anastasia Codd Moore.

1784 Attended private school run by T. J. Malone.

1786 Attended English Grammar School; Samuel Whyte, headmaster of "the best school in Dublin."

1790 First stage appearance, speaking epilogue to *Jane Shore* in private theatricals.

1793 October, first appeared in print with verses in *Anthologia Hibernica*, Dublin magazine.

1794 June, attended Dr. Carr's Latin School, preparatory to Trinity College, Dublin.

1795 January, entered Trinity; tried for scholarship but as Roman Catholic was ineligible. Began translation of Anacreon. Robert Emmet and Edward Hudson were fellow students and friends.

1798 May, rebellion of United Irishmen. Emmet, who had left college in April, was wounded but survived; Hudson was imprisoned and exiled; Wolfe Tone died in prison, allegedly a suicide; Lord Edward Fitzgerald died of wounds. Moore was questioned but refused to testify against his friends; permitted to remain in college.

1799 March, received B.A. degree from Trinity. April to July, read law in Middle Temple, London; never admitted to bar. Worked on *Anacreon*. Returned to Dublin. (This was his first trip to England.)

1800 *Odes of Anacreon* (London).

1801 *The Poetical Works of Thomas Little, Jr.* (London).

1802 July 27, *The Gypsy Prince*, opera, for which Moore wrote part of libretto, performed at Haymarket Theater, London.

1803 Declined offer of Irish Laureateship, created for him. Robert Emmet hanged. Moore appointed registrar of admiralty prize-court, Bermuda; September, sailed for Norfolk, Virginia; arrived in November.

1804 January 3, sailed for Bermuda. April, appointed deputy to take over duties; sailed for New York. Traveled in eastern United States and Canada. October, sailed for England.

1806 *Epistles, Odes, and Other Poems* (London). Denounced by Francis Jeffrey in *Edinburgh Review;* challenged Jeffrey to duel, which was stopped by police; they were reconciled and became lifelong friends.

1808 First and second volumes of *Irish Melodies* (London and Dublin); series continued to Volume 10 in 1834.

1811 March 25, married Elizabeth (Bessy) Dyke, London. Lived in England thereafter.

1812 February 4, daughter Barbara born. Moved to Kegworth, Leicestershire. Began contributing to *Morning Chronicle.*

1813 March 16, daughter Anastasia born. Moved to Mayfield, Derbyshire. *Intercepted Letters, or The Two-Penny Post-Bag* (London).

1814 Began contributing to *Edinburgh Review.* August 18, daughter Olivia born.

1815 Spring, daughter Olivia died. Moore in Ireland until autumn.

1816 First volume of *Sacred Songs* (London and Dublin); Volume 2 out in 1824.

1817 *Lalla Rookh* (London). Visit to France. September 17, daughter Barbara died after a fall.

1818 *The Fudge Family in Paris* ("by Thomas Brown the Younger") (London). First volume of *National Airs* published (London and Dublin); series continued to Volume 6 in 1827. Moved to Sloperton Cottage, near Bowood, Wiltshire, his home for the remainder of his life. October 24, son Thomas born.

1819 Deputy in Bermuda absconded with £6000, for which Moore was responsible. To avoid arrest for debt, went to Continent. May, traveled in Switzerland and Italy; saw Byron for last time and was given manuscript of Byron's Memoirs. Family joined him in Paris at end of year. First collected volume, *The Works of Thomas Moore* (six volumes) published (Paris).

1822   November, returned to England after compromise settlement of debt.

1823   *The Loves of the Angels* and *Fables for the Holy Alliance* (by "Thomas Brown the Younger") (London). May 24, son Russell born. In Ireland wtih Lansdowne.

1824   *Memoirs of Captain Rock* (London). Dispute over burning of Byron's memoirs.

1825   *Memoirs of the Life of the Right Honourable Richard Brinsley Sheridan* (London). Visit to Sir Walter Scott in Edinburgh. December 17, father died; Moore in Ireland.

1826   *Evenings in Greece* (London).

1827   *The Epicurean: A Tale* (London).

1828   *Odes upon Cash, Corn, Catholics, and Other Matters* (London).

1829   March 18, daughter Anastasia died. Catholic Emancipation Bill passed.

1830   *Letters and Journals of Lord Byron, with Notices of His Life* (London).

1831   *The Life and Death of Lord Fitzgerald* (London).

1832   May 18, mother died.

1833   *Travels of an Irish Gentleman in Search of a Religion* (London).

1834   December, sister Catherine (Kate) died.

1835   First volume of *History of Ireland* (London) (Volume 4 [last], 1846). *The Fudge Family in England* (London). Granted Civil List pension, £300 a year. Triumphal visit to Ireland; elected to British Association for the Advancement of Science.

1838   Last visit to Ireland.

1841   *The Poetical Works of Thomas Moore, Collected by Himself* (ten volumes) (London), with autobiographical preface to each volume.

1842   Received Order of Merit from Frederick the Great of Prussia. November 23, son Russell died.

1846   February, son Thomas and sister Ellen died. Moore's health failed from this time on.

1849   Moore lapsed into senile dementia.

1852   February 25, Moore died.

CHAPTER 1

The Man and His Life

I *The Making of a Writer*

THE Ireland into which Thomas Moore[1] was born on May 28, 1779, was a land of depression and decay. Though official union with England did not come until 1800, the Protestant Anglo-Irish minority was in complete control. The overwhelming majority, the native Irish population, was Roman Catholic by religion, and was, for the most part, made up of tenant farmers at the mercy of their (frequently absentee) landlords. Catholics had no right to vote, to hold office, to serve on juries, to educate their children, to engage in most of the professions, or to bear arms. They had to pay a tithe of their wretched subsistence to support the established Anglican Church. Moore's birth was not registered because Catholic births were not; instead, his mother had a medal cast to commemorate the date.

The natural result of this oppression was a series of revolts, organized and unorganized, necessarily conspiratorial. No Catholic Irishman, even the relatively few in the lower middle class who managed to keep above the level of starvation, could be expected to acquiesce meekly to the iron despotism under which he lived. "I was born a rebel," Moore said—though by reason of physique and temperament his rebellion was always one of words, not deeds. "He walked on the sunny side of the street, but he was faithful." [2]

Nevertheless, his childhood was an indulged and happy one. He was the oldest child of John Moore, whose Leinster ancestors had some claim to the aristocratic prefix "O'," and of Anastasia Codd Moore. The Codds were originally an English Protestant family which after several generations in County Kerry had become Roman Catholics. Both parents were unusual people. The father was a provision merchant (a grocer), and the family lived above the shop at 12 Aungier Street in Dublin. "I love Ireland,"

Thomas Moore was to say, "but I hate Dublin." He had no reason to do so; Dublin was always very good to him.

Hardly more than a nominal Catholic, John Moore was easygoing, tolerant, and rather anticlerical. Anastasia was more devout, but she was also a highly intelligent woman with a taste for the arts and with immense ambition, which became centered on her precocious little son. It was from his mother that Thomas derived his musical talent—and it was also from her that he learned his desire for social recognition, a need which earned him the jibe that he "dearly loved a lord." He did; but he discriminated among them. Henry Hazlitt, who was a Tory, sneered that "he fancies himself one of the set to which he is admitted on sufferance," [3] but that is not true; Moore's titled friends loved him and considered him at least their equal.

Two sisters, Catherine (Kate) and Ellen, were born after him; and there seem to have been three other children who died in infancy. It was an affectionate family, and Moore was devoted to them all, but to his mother most of all.

When Thomas was five, he was sent to a private Classical English School run by T. S. Malone, who appears to have been a brilliant scholar but also an alcoholic who whipped his pupils if they woke him by coming to school before noon! Nevertheless, Thomas learned enough from him to win a silver medal for history at six; at seven his parents took him away and enrolled him in what was considered "the best school in Dublin," the English Grammar School, of which Samuel Whyte, a really great teacher, was headmaster. Shortly after Moore's birth, the restrictions on educating Irish Catholic boys had been considerably eased (though still severe); in fact, by the time he was four, Catholics had become eligible for Trinity College, his future *alma mater*—although they could not receive scholarships. Fortunately, John Moore was prosperous enough to be able to afford the best education available for his son.

Between a mother who was so eager for him to become learned that she would wake him at one or two in the morning to hear his lessons, and a teacher who recognized his ability and rapidly made him his favorite pupil, young Thomas soon led his class and laid the foundations of a good knowledge of Greek and Latin. Later he became fluent also in French and Italian. In a letter to

Tom's father, Whyte spoke of him as "your incomparable boy." [4]

Whyte was not only a schoolmaster; he was also a poet, or at least a versifier; he loved music; and he was passionately fond of the stage. His pupils, and Moore most of all, followed him into all of these interests. They were nothing new for Moore; from earliest childhood he had been encouraged to recite, sing, and play the harpsichord and the piano-forte (as pianos were then called). He was eleven when he made his first theatrical appearance, reciting the epilogue to a play about Jane Shore (mistress of Edward IV) at one of the amateur dramatic performances which were the rage in Dublin. If he had any plans for the future, he expected to be an actor.

But literature won out over the theater. He was fourteen when he first saw himself in print—in a new literary magazine called *Anthologia Hibernica* (Irish Anthology), with verses addressed to one Zelia "on her charging the author with writing too much of love"! (Zelia was a spinster twice his age.) More interestingly, the magazine also had some Masonic connections, but his tolerant parents made no objection to his writing for it. They, his little sisters, and his teachers all doted on him; he could easily have become a spoiled little show-off, but in fact he was never spoiled, his nature remained friendly and outgoing, and under his patent vanity was a basic modesty. (In evidence, he dropped all these overpraised juvenile poems from his *Collected Poetical Works*.)

In June, 1794, at fifteen, he was transferred to Dr. Carr's Latin School, a sort of cramming school in preparation for Trinity. The following January he entered the college. The Latin School sent his name in marked "Protestant"; when he discovered this, he had it changed, thus making himself ineligible for the scholarship for which he had passed the examination with high marks.

Moore did not work very hard at Trinity on the set courses of his prescribed curriculum. There were too many distractions. For one thing, he had begun his translation of the Greek verses attributed to Anacreon, an effort which was published in 1800. For another, among his fellow students who became his friends were at least two—Robert Emmet and Edward Hudson—who were deeply involved with the group of revolutionaries known as the United Irishmen.

Both Hudson and Emmet realized how unfit this undersized

[15]

romantic dreamer was for the grim business of armed revolt. They told him little—not because they did not trust him, but because they did not want to implicate him—and they discouraged his active participation in their plot. But Moore, the "born rebel," could not help being fired by what he heard or guessed. One result was an inflammatory "Letter to the Students of Trinity College" published in December, 1797, in *The Press*, a paper issued by the United Irishmen to oppose the imminent Act of Union with England. It was signed "A SOPHister," but both Moore's parents and his tutor knew who the author was, and his mother implored him not to endanger his whole future by further publications of this kind. There were repercussions the next year, which eventuated in one of Thomas Moore's finest moments.

The open revolt of the United Irishmen was at hand. It is not possible here to give any adequate account of this part of Irish history, except in so far as it affected Moore and his subsequent writing on Irish questions. Briefly, we must remember that not only Ireland was in a fever of rebellion in this era. It was the time of the French Revolution and the Napoleonic Wars that followed; the American Revolution had been successful only a score of years before. The United Irishmen began as a counter-organization to the milder nationalism of Henry Grattan; but Wolfe Tone, its leader, was a disciple of the French Jacobins, and gradually what had been a democratic movement of patriotic Irishmen, Catholic and Protestant alike, striving to secure reform, became a conspiracy for an armed rebellion to bring about an Irish Republic. In April, 1798, Emmet withdrew from Trinity. The rebellion took place in May. It was a total failure and was brutally crushed. Wolfe Tone died in prison—the authorities claimed by his own hand; Lord Edward Fitzgerald died of his wounds; Hudson was imprisoned and exiled; Emmet was wounded but survived to be hanged in another outbreak five years later.

Amid the furor, Trinity set up an inquisition, since its own students were involved; and Moore was summoned to testify. It is doubtful if the investigators knew of his authorship of the "Letter," but Emmet and Hudson were among his close friends. His graduation from college and his entire future were at stake. At first the nineteen-year-old boy refused to take the oath at all; finally he consented to do so, but announced in advance that under no condition would he answer questions about anyone but himself. (It is the same stand that has been taken by so many witnesses before Congressional committees in this country.) Moore had no desire to be a hero, but he had integrity and he was not a coward. The investigators were impressed; he won his point and was permitted to remain in college.

In March, 1799, not yet quite twenty years old, he received his Bachelor of Arts degree from Trinity; and by April he was in London—his first trip away from Ireland. He was entered in the Middle Temple to read for the bar, but if he carried out any study of the law, it must have been nominal. He spent most of his time making useful friends and finishing his translation of Anacreon. His legal career, such as it was, lasted just three months. In July he returned home.

Moore was at this time on the verge of his serious literary vocation. Nearly all its components were already in the making. The *Odes of Anacreon,* which first brought him wide attention, was to appear the next year; and thanks to Edward Hudson, he had already become interested in the old Irish bardic songs, before the last of the traditional harpists had perished. That interest was to end in the *Irish Melodies* and make him "the voice of Ireland."

II *"Anacreon Moore"*

The light, frivolous poems from or after Anacreon created a sensation. In the circles he valued, Moore became known as "Anacreon Moore." When in the next year he brought out the pseudonymous *Poetical Works of Thomas Little, Esq.,* made up of sentimental and artificial juvenilia, his reputation and popularity spread still more widely. Thomas Little's identity was an open secret, and London society and the less ponderous of the literati found Moore enormously to their taste. The violent condemnations of staid, right-wing critics only added to their acclaim.

Back home in Dublin, and still more on his occasional visits to London, Moore was beginning to meet people of rank and influence. He came to know them not only through his writings, but, in the beginning at least, through his musical and theatrical appearances. Without connections, in that era of patronage, any successful literary career by an "outsider," such as Moore was, was quite impossible. His principal noble patron at this time was the (Irish) Earl of Moira, formerly Lord Rawdon, later the Marquis of Hastings. Moira served with distinction both in the American war and later in India; between these two periods he was at home in Ireland and a power in the Whiggish advocacy of Catholic Emancipation.

Moore met Lord Moira through Captain Joseph Atkinson, secretary of the Irish Ordnance Board and the center of cultural— and especially of theatrical—life in Dublin; Atkinson had served under Moira in America. Moira shared Atkinson's admiration of the young poet and in some sense became his sponsor—giving rise to expectations of patronage that were not fulfilled. Probably Moira's early interest was further aroused by Moore's contribution of songs and part of the libretto for a light opera called *The Gypsy Prince* which was performed with success in London in 1802. (Moore himself was displeased with the production and vowed he would never write for opera again, and he never did: *M.P., or the Blue-Stocking* was more of a play with interspersed songs.)

By way of encouraging their young protégé, Moira and Atkinson put their heads together and wangled the creation of an Irish Laureateship for his benefit. To their surprise Moore declined the honor and whatever emoluments went with it—and that was the beginning and the end of any idea of an Irish Poet Laureate. He remained completely level-headed in the midst of growing adulation, and undoubtedly realized how ridiculous such a post would seem in his twenty-fourth year. (Later, when he was incontestably "The Bard," he would perhaps have accepted it.) The immense success of *Anacreon* had not blinded him to the fact that he was at the commencement, not the climax or the conclusion, of his poetic accomplishment.

What he did anticipate from Moira was some well-paying nominal governmental post—the most usual means by which those high in the ruling political party rewarded aspiring clients without private incomes. To Moore's disappointment, all that Moira was able to bestow upon him before he left for India was an appointment as registrar of the admiralty prize-court in far-away Bermuda. It was a sinecure, but it did not keep him in either Dublin or London.

Disappointed or not, Moore could hardly refuse. On September 25, 1803, he sailed for Norfolk, Virginia, there being no direct passage to Bermuda. He arrived in Norfolk in November—a quick trip for those times.

It was the year in which Robert Emmet was hanged. But there was nothing unseemly in Moore's acceptance of office under the British government which had hanged his old friend. Patriotic Irishman as he always was, his devotion to his country was romantic, the attachment of a dreamer and a poet. Essentially, in our modern terms, he was a middle-of-the-road liberal. He had no first-hand knowledge of the downtrodden peasants until much later; all his life his associations had been with the more enlightened of the Irish gentry. He never advocated complete severance from England; William F. P. Stockley hit near to the truth when he said in effect that Moore's advice to his compatriots came to this: "Trust England in the future and hope for Ireland." [5] He was an Irish patriot—but one who idealized both Ireland and England.

For two months Moore stayed with the British Consul in Norfolk; then in January he went at last to Bermuda. He did not stay long. His duties were negligible, and the dull life of a colonial bureaucrat was not for him. He took a house in St. George (later a commercialized "shrine"); he carried on a flirtation with a young lady he called Nea (a Miss Hester Louise Tucker), to whom he addressed saccharine poems in the "Thomas Little" style; and then in April he appointed a deputy to carry on what work there was, put him in charge, and left the island. This deputy resigned later, and Moore appointed another, a man named Sheddon—much to his subsequent grief.

Before returning to England, Moore spent nine months touring the eastern United States and Canada. He did not like what he saw in the former country. How much he had been influenced unconsciously by his experience as the petted darling of the more culture-conscious aristocracy came out in the verses—his first satire—he wrote during this, his only visit to America. The rough-and-ready United States of 1804 offended and disgusted him. Only the Philadelphia Federalists and the loyal Canadians pleased him. Understandably he was revolted by the crudity of the average provincial American—much as Mrs. Trollope and

Dickens were to be affected later on. He met his old Trinity friend Edward Hudson again, but was alienated by Hudson's adherence to democratic views. It was a temporary aberration; Moore was not a snob or a reactionary, and he was apologetic afterwards: but the fact remains that he detested nearly all he saw in America.[6]

In October he set sail again for England. He was welcomed back into the circles where he was half-friend, half-entertainer. Little Moore—with his curly black hair; his dark, nearsighted eyes; and his sweet small tenor voice—was becoming more than the favorite of a group of noble Whig politicians: he had a sure place by this time in the literary world as well. It was the period in which Gerald Griffin, the Irish novelist, called Moore "a neat-made little fellow, . . . finished as an actor, but without an actor's affectation; easy as a gentleman, but without some gentlemen's formality; in a word . . . a hospitable warm-hearted Irishman."

Samuel Rogers, then highly regarded as a poet and famous for his literary breakfasts, was his close friend and his constant host; he met Wordsworth and Coleridge and Southey and Lamb not so much on terms of friendship as of amiable condescension to them. He was "Anacreon Moore," and far better known than they to the general public.

It was in this aura that he published his *Epistles, Odes, and Other Poems*—sentimental, frivolous, and (for the time) rather naughty. "Society" loved them, although careful mamas kept them from their unmarried daughters. And they fell foul of the shocked indignation of the mighty *Edinburgh Review*. Francis Jeffrey, afterwards Lord Jeffrey, the editor, denounced them and their author in such violent terms that Moore, outraged and always touchy about any impingement on his honor, challenged Jeffrey to a duel.

The duel became a farce. While they waited for their seconds to load the pistols, the principals, who took to each other at sight, exchanged amiable witticisms. When at last the seconds were ready, the police suddenly arrived and stopped the affair; and when the pistols were examined at police headquarters (or the 1806 equivalent) one of them was found to be devoid of bullets! Actually, both had been loaded but the bullets had fallen out. There was a great deal of ridicule in the Tory press about this business, and Moore was all his life very thin-skinned on the subject.

He and Jeffrey became intimate friends thereafter; Moore became a contributor to the *Edinburgh Review* and later declined an offer to be its editor. Then Byron, in *English Bards and Scotch Reviewers,* repeated the jeering calumny; and as soon as he was within reaching distance, Moore challenged him also. Byron replied in a conciliatory manner, Rogers brought them together (they had never met previously), and Byron too, with momentous consequences, became his devoted friend.

III *"Melody Moore"*

Moore had become well-known as the author of popular love-poems in the pseudoclassic, sentimental manner. Then came, unwittingly, the greatest opportunity of his life. The Power brothers, publishers, James in London and William in Dublin, proposed that he write words to the tunes of the old Irish folk songs taken down a few years before at the last convocation of the traditional country harpists. Sir John Stevenson was to arrange the airs. The collection eventually grew to ten volumes.

Moore was ideally suited for this task. All his patriotic fervor, his romantic idealization of Irish history, his turn for melodious verse, his musical ear, and his high capacity for experimental metrical technique fitted him for just such an assignment. He knew not a word of Gaelic—he never did—and probably the original words fitted to the tunes bore no relation whatever to the ones he wrote. But the *Irish Melodies* burst on the reading public of both Ireland and England (and even on the public which merely listened, for part of Moore's contract was to sing his own songs at innumerable private gatherings) like a poetic revelation.

"Anacreon Moore" became "Melody Moore." He was the Bard of Ireland, as Shakespeare was the Bard of England. Not even Byron had awakened to find himself so famous.

It is a marvel that his head was not completely turned. But it was not. He remained what he had always been—a man easily flattered but never swell-headed, socially aspiring but never servile, a bit pedantic but truly erudite, an Irish patriot but at the same time an associate of the English Whigs. (He was never himself a Whig; he endorsed the Whigs as friends of Ireland.) He was still Tom Moore—touchily independent and careful of his honor, hard-working, friendly, and full of charm.

Like every other human being, Moore was the child of his time and place. Much that he wrote is practically unreadable now, but the enormous acclamation given him was not altogether unde-served. For three quarters of a century more English-reading men (and especially women) read and loved Moore than ever read Keats or Shelley or Wordsworth; and even today older people, at least, know many of the *Irish Melodies* as familiar songs—even though they may never have known who wrote the words to them.

The first two volumes of the *Irish Melodies* came out in 1808. They continued to be Moore's chief literary task—and, except for his Bermuda income, were his chief source of livelihood for some years to come. When the Power brothers quarreled and separated, the *Irish Melodies* were published by James Power in London and were pirated by brother William in Dublin. Moore, of course, kept on writing verse in other veins, but his next major work did not appear until 1814. It was his first great success as a satirist, *Intercepted Letters, or the Two-Penny Post-Bag*—although it had been preceded by a number of polemic and satirical political pieces in both verse and prose. During those six years a great deal happened in Moore's personal life.

Private theatricals were still the rage in Ireland as in England. Moore was one of a group which put on plays in Kilkenny; the male parts were taken by the gentleman amateurs, but profes-sional actresses were engaged from Dublin for the female roles. Among these were three sisters named Dyke, the daughters of an English dancing-master and puppeteer. Moore acted and sang in many of the performances, and of course met the sisters. On March 25, 1811, Thomas Moore and Elizabeth Dyke were mar-ried by special license in London—in St. Martin's, an Anglican church.

In his poems, Moore had been a butterfly, flitting from flower to flower, sipping their honey at random. In life, he had flirted tre-mendously and probably had done a bit of philandering; but ap-parently he had done little more. At thirty-two, he may have been almost as virginal as his sixteen-year-old bride. (There is some doubt about Bessy's exact age; she herself thought she was a year and a half older than her baptismal certificate shows her to have been.)

Very often in their long marriage, Bessy stayed at home in the country with the children while her husband was the ornament of the dinner tables of lords in their country houses and of celebrities in London. But that implied no neglect: social life was a function of his career as a professional writer. Besides, Bessy was shy and the children kept her tied down. Moore was always delighted to get back to the peace of his rural home and Bessy's company. Their marriage remained a love-match, idyllic and devoted. He was a concerned and tender husband and father, as deeply attached to wife and children as to his parents and sisters in Ireland. From that time on, Moore lived permanently in England; Ireland became a place he visited.

On February 4, 1812, his daughter Barbara was born; and on March 16, 1813, a second daughter, Anastasia, who was named for his mother. The Moores moved about from one rented cottage to another, always near the seat—and hence the necessary reference library—of one of the great Whig landowners who were his friends. In an age of lordly patronage of the creative artist (by way of governmental benefices), all Moore had received was his small income, minus the deputy's share, from the Bermuda post. He earned his living by writing, and much of the writing was in effect journalism. He began contributing to the *Edinburgh Review* the same year that *Intercepted Letters* appeared, and later he wrote constantly for two London newspapers, *The Times* and *The Morning Chronicle*. To the outward eye he might seem to have been perpetually engaged in singing his songs (to his own rather inept accompaniment) in drawing rooms, or exchanging witty repartee at dinner parties; but we know from his journal that the greater part of his time was spent at his writing table or walking up and down in his garden, which was his habit during poetic creation. He earned a fortune from his writing; yet although he was scrupulous, he was a poor financier, always in debt to his publishers for advances; and he could never afford to turn down a lucrative offer.[7]

A third daughter, Olivia (whose godfather was Byron) was born on August 18, 1814, but died the following spring. Moore, who was always terribly shaken by illness or death among those he loved, recovered from the impact of the loss by making a long visit to Ireland. The *Irish Melodies* kept on appearing, volume after volume; and in 1816 he published the first volume of *Sacred Songs*. These were hymns, some written to tunes by Haydn, more to those by Sir John Stevenson, Moore himself, and sundry unknown composers.

IV   *The Author of* Lalla Rookh

Thomas Moore had been "Anacreon Moore" and "Melody Moore," and also the author of comic squibs, satires, and pungent political verses. His versatility was far from its end. In 1817 *Lalla Rookh* burst upon the world like a benignant bomb.

This series of four narrative poems interspersed with prose—pseudo-Oriental, lush, and semi-Byronic (though actually written, if not published, before either *The Giaour* or *The Bride of Abydos*)—catapulted Moore from "Irish Bard" to the idol of what would now be called the middle-brow public. *Lalla Rookh* went into innumerable editions; it was translated into almost every literate tongue, including Persian, whence it allegedly sprang; everything was named for it, from ships to ice cream; girls—a few of whom, named for great-grandmothers, are still living—were christened Lalla. Everything from or about the Near East became the raging fashion of the time. It was Moore's great fortune in his own lifetime—and his misfortune in ours—to be exactly fitted to his era. Not even Byron meant as much to his first readers as Moore in his heyday meant to his.

Exhausted by the labor of this immense poem, for which he had done an enormous amount of research, Moore went to France to recuperate. He was called home by word that his first born, five-year-old Barbara, had been badly injured in a fall. She died on September 17. His journal records the agony he underwent—and, as in later deaths, his shrinking from being present at the death-bed. It was Bessy, courageous and loving and well aware of the melancholy lurking under her husband's gaiety, who insisted on going through that ordeal alone.[8]

For Moore 1818 was a momentous year. The family moved to Sloperton Cottage, in Wiltshire, near the country seat of another of his close friends, Lord Lansdowne.[9] It was Moore's home for the remainder of his life. There his first son, Thomas, was born on

October 24. In that same year the first volume of a new song series, *National Airs* (meaning tunes of several different nations)
appeared, and was followed by the gay and witty *Fudge Family
in Paris* (by "Thomas Brown the Younger")—perhaps the best,
and certainly the most readable, of his satirical poems. It was well
that this was a year of success and happiness, for the next year
brought disaster.

Moore apparently paid little attention to his continuing post in
Bermuda, except to receive the income from it. So it was a shock
when he learned the deputy, Sheddon, had absconded with
£6000 in government funds for which the registrar was responsible. There was, of course, no shadow of criminality on Moore's
part; and he was in hopes that Sheddon's prosperous relatives
might make good some of his defalcation. It was impossible for
him to pay this sum at once; he was always behind in advances
from his publishers, and his only way to make such an amount
was by more writing and more advances. Meanwhile he faced a
debtor's prison, where he would not have been able to earn
money at all. He did the wisest thing under the circumstances; he
took the advice of his more worldly friends and left for France.
For a few months he traveled with Lord John Russell (father of
the Reform Bill, and Bertrand Russell's grandfather) in France,
Switzerland, and Italy. In Venice, Moore saw Byron for the last
time; and when they parted, Byron gave him his manuscript
memoirs, with the agreement that Moore was free to have them
published after his friend's death. This agreement was to become
another source of trouble.

Moore settled in Paris, and that is why his first collected volume, consisting of all his more important work up to that date,
appeared under a French imprint. At the end of the year Bessy
and the children joined him. Except for a brief surreptitious trip
to England and Ireland, slightly disguised and under an alias, he
remained in exile until November, 1822. (He was therefore in
France when Shelley was drowned in Italy, and one wonders if he
knew of it. He was one of the few of the time who had great
respect for Shelley's poetry.)

At last Moore learned that, partly by a £300 repayment by a
relative of Sheddon's, the debt had been reduced to £740, and
that unknown to him Lord Lansdowne had paid that. Moore re-

paid Lansdowne at once, by a draft on Longmans, his publisher, and gratefully returned with the family to Sloperton Cottage. There he set to work on a new major poem. The continuing volumes of the various song series brought him only a small, if steady, income; and he had constantly to keep producing other larger works.

The Loves of the Angels, made up of three connected poems embodying the confessions of three fallen seraphs who had become enamored of mortal women, came out in 1823. The book, if not so overwhelmingly popular as *Lalla Rookh,* at least was a "best seller." There was considerable objection to its theme from shocked orthodox Christians; so from the fifth edition on, after some further research resulting in a new flock of footnotes, the angels became Mohammedans! Later in that year the satirical *Fables for the Holy Alliance* was published—like *The Fudge Family in Paris,* under the pseudonym of "Thomas Brown the Younger." Of course everybody, including the indignant Tory press, knew that Moore was the author. On May 24 his second son and last child (John) Russell, named for Lord Russell, was born.

In 1824 Moore's first considerable prose volume, the fictitious "memoirs" of the mythical Captain Rock, a sort of Irish folk hero who attacked the landlords and their holdings on behalf of the desperate peasants, appeared and was greeted with wild enthusiasm in Irish revolutionary circles and with feelings strictly determined by political sympathies in England. The book rose from Moore's burning indignation over his first glimpse of what he called the real "Irish misery and filth." He had visited Ireland with Lord Lansdowne in 1823; and though the Lansdownes themselves were good landlords, Moore had seen with horror what peasant life was like under many others who were not.

V *The Biographer*

But 1824 was memorable in Moore's life for quite another reason than the publication of *Captain Rock.* It was the year of the miserable dispute over Byron's memoirs, which Byron had given him and had supplemented by sending him an additional manuscript afterwards. This free gift aroused the jealousy of the man who claimed to be Byron's most intimate friend, John Cam Hobhouse, who asserted that Byron had regretted his impulsive act and would have withdrawn it except for fear of hurting Moore's feelings. Moreover, both the estranged Lady Byron and Byron's beloved half-sister, Augusta Leigh, were uneasy at Moore's possession of what might well be indiscreet or scandalous memoirs. Neither of them knew Moore, and neither of them was among his admirers. Moore had lent the manuscript, rather imprudently, to one or two of his acquaintances; but he always insisted that there was nothing in it to alarm anyone.

The whole story is too complex to be told briefly; Doris Langley Moore (no relation) has written a book on it entitled *The Late Lord Byron*. To sum it up, Byron died in Greece on April 19, 1824. The memoirs were then in the hands of the publisher John Murray, for a loan to Moore of two thousand guineas. The original deed of sale had stipulated that either Byron or Moore could redeem the manuscript; and Moore thought, mistakenly, that he had three months' grace after Byron died. He had been on the point of repaying Murray because Longmans were offering more for the publication. Actually by this time Murray was the legal owner.

Then Lady Byron (through Douglas Kinnaird) and Mrs. Leigh (through Hobhouse) stepped in, each demanding the right to redeem the manuscript and to decide whether it should be published or destroyed. In the end, out-talked and anxious lest his honor and integrity be impugned, Moore gave in; and the memoirs were burned unread in Murray's fireplace. That left him two thousand guineas in debt to Murray—which is why Murray became the publisher of the biography of Byron, unquestionably Moore's best work in prose. Murray was reimbursed from its proceeds, for neither Lady Byron nor Mrs. Leigh ever paid anything. Everybody acted from the highest motives, but no one will ever know now how much was lost of our knowledge of Byron's life and character.

Before Moore could begin work on the Byron biography, he had to finish a biography of Richard Brinsley Sheridan, the dramatist; for he was under contract with Longmans to do so. Sheridan had died in 1816, and Moore had begun the book in 1819. It was interrupted by his years of exile in France, when he could not interview Sheridan's associates or consult the family papers; accordingly it did not appear until 1825. That was the year in which his father died; Moore hurried to Dublin at the news of his illness but as usual absented himself from the deathbed. John Moore died in December. Earlier in 1825 Moore had rested from his exhausting labor on the Sheridan biography by making his only journey to Scotland and visiting Sir Water Scott at Abbotsford. Despite their political differences, the two, who for so many reasons might have been expected to be antagonistic, took to each other at once and remained fast friends for the remaining years of Scott's life. (Scott's rather curious encomium was that Moore had "not the least touch of the poet or the pedant.") Still there was unfinished work to be done before Moore could begin the gigantic task of editing Byron's letters and journals and writing the "notices" of his life. *Evenings in Greece,* among the more negligible of Moore's poem series, appeared in 1826; the powerfully satiric *Odes upon Cash, Corn, Catholics, and Other Matters,* and *The Epicurean,* this only seminovel (outgrowth of an unfinished narrative poem, *Alciphron*), in 1828. Then at last he was able to settle down to the biography of Byron, the material for which was overwhelming. The book did not appear until 1830.

In 1829 the Catholic Emancipation Bill was signed at last; and so far as Moore the writer was concerned, it eventuated four years later in *Travels of an Irish Gentleman in Search of a Religion.* But for Moore the man and father, 1829 was shadowed by the death (from the after-effects of measles) of his beloved and only remaining daughter, Anastasia, at sixteen. Again his journal shows how he suffered. Anastasia's last words were for him, but he could not bring himself to hear them; he paced his study while brave, understanding Bessy, by her own insistence, stayed alone to watch their child die.

The shadows were beginning to close in. Moore kept on working. Despite the vast sums he earned, and though he always lived frugally, his financial burdens were heavy. The family in Dublin was now largely dependent on him. Long before John Moore died, he had lost to retirement on half pay the modest job as barrack master which his son had obtained for him in 1815; and thus Thomas's mother and sisters became his full charge. It was a period when to the outward eye Thomas Moore was still the gay singer at aristocratic soirees, the life of the party at gatherings of the literati. In actuality he was a man of fifty, old before his time,

gray and balding, growing very tired, but indomitably cheerful
before the public gaze. He confided only to his journal how much
he preferred life in the country with his family, how he longed
more and more to escape from London to his "sweet garden and
study."

Before he had even finished the immense task on *The Letters
and Journals of Lord Byron, with Notices of His Life,* he was
already at work on a biography of Lord Edward Fitzgerald, the
Irish rebel of those early days in Trinity College, Fitzgerald had
died of his wounds in the revolt of the United Irishmen. That
book came out a year after the Byron biography in 1831. The
Reform Bill finally passed that year, but things were going too
quickly for Moore's middle-of-the-road views. In 1832 he was
asked to stand for Parliament for Limerick and was assured of
election, but he declined. His interest in politics was coming to an
end, and the Fitzgerald book was almost his last written expression on the Irish question.

VI   *The Last Years*

In May, 1832, Moore's mother died.[10] Moore did not get to Ireland in time to see her alive. His sister Kate, who had long been
an invalid, followed her in December, 1834. Moore's only major
publication of those two years was the *Travels of an Irish Gentleman in Search of a Religion,* in 1833: *The Fudge Family in England,* which fell rather flat, appeared in 1835. Then Moore was left
face to face with what proved to be his last book (except for his
collected poems)—a book which helped to subject him to a living
death, if not to kill him: the massive four-volume *History of Ireland.* It was a work utterly unsuited to his talents and turn of
mind. He was not a historian; he had no idea of the requirements
for a definitive history. He said justly that for the first time in his
life he felt like a hack writer. But he had contracted to write the
book; he had been paid for it; and after a feeble attempt to get
out of it, he labored on doggedly until it was finished. By the time
the last volume was done, in 1846, he was so utterly worn out and
broken under personal sorrows that he no longer had the energy
to write a preface for it and had to ask the publisher to assign the
task to someone else.

But the sun that was beginning to sink still shed a few beneficent rays. George IV, whom, as the Regent, Moore had flattered when the prince was amiably inclined toward Ireland, and had hated and excoriated when he failed to redeem his promises, had died in 1830. He had been succeeded by his brother, who as William IV was more amenable. The Whigs were in power again, and Moore at last received a Civil List pension of £300 a year in 1835, with another £100 added later for the education of his sons. The benefaction did not go unopposed.[11]

This was also the year of his most triumphal visit to Ireland, when he was almost mobbed by his admirers, was feted everywhere, and was greeted exultantly when he attended the theater. In short, Moore was given the same kind of adoring welcome that nowadays is accorded only to singers of a very different sort! One rather odd honor he received was election by acclamation to the British Association for the Advancement of Science, which was meeting in Dublin—even though he had never shown the slightest interest in scientific questions. The next year he made his last journey to his native land, and it was almost as great a tour of triumph. In 1841 his collected *Poetical Works*, in ten volumes, was published with an autobiographical preface to each volume; but these covered only his early years. Nevertheless, except for his journal and correspondence, published after his death, this affords the only first-hand information we have about him. It is also the last work of any consequence that he did. As a poet he was still internationally famous. A year later he received the Order of Merit from that constant celebrity-hunter, Frederick the Great of Prussia.

The rest of the story is sad, and needs little telling. It began with the older son, Thomas, a spoiled, extravagant, utterly irresponsible youth. His father had, as Thomas desired, and at great sacrifice, bought him a commission in the Army. Young Tom was stationed in Dublin, got into some kind of trouble, fell ill, was sent to India, and fell ill again there. In both places he got badly into debt and had to be ransomed with much difficulty by his father. Then without warning he sold his commission. Moore's favorite sister Ellen was seriously ill. He was still struggling with the *History of Ireland*. The younger boy, Russell, was more satisfactory in character, but delicate in health. He too went out to India, to a civil post in Bengal, where it was discovered that he had tuberculosis. He was invalided home in 1842, lingered until November, and died.

Young Tom next turned up in France, where he fell in love and announced that he wished to enter the French Army. His father managed to secure him an appointment as *sous-lieutenant* in the Foreign Legion, and he was posted in North Africa. There he ran into trouble again, and begged his father for fifty pounds to "keep him out of prison." His father did not have the money to send him. Tom apparently did not go to prison, but the next news was that he was ill of a fever. That was in 1845. In February, 1846, Ellen died in Dublin, and a month later Moore received word that his last child had died in Africa.

Even Bessy almost succumbed to this last blow, and Moore never fully recovered from it. For a long time, although he was only in his sixties, he had begun to show symptoms of premature senility. His memory failed badly, and several times, in the midst of delighting his hearers with singing of one of the *Irish Melodies,* he had been seized with hysterical fits of sobbing. He fell ill with what was called influenza, and his recovery was slow. After he finished the *History of Ireland* he was quite unable to work, except for desultory entries in his journal, and then even that ended. "I am sinking into a mere vegetable," he wrote in a letter. Then, one day in 1849, while he was sitting with his two friends Russell and Lansdowne, he suddenly lapsed into senile dementia. For the two years or so that his body remained alive, he recognized no one, except occasionally Bessy. Once in a while he tried quaveringly to sing one of the old songs. Like Swift's more powerful brain, his had fallen to imbecility. On February 25, 1852, at six o'clock in the evening, he slipped quietly into death.

Always calling himself and thinking of himself as a Roman Catholic, Moore had yet married a Protestant in a Protestant church, had reared his children as Protestants, and was buried in a Protestant graveyard. His true religion was, as W. F. P. Stockley says, "a sentimental pietistic Deism." [12] He wrote to Byron: "I would not give up the *poetry* of religion for all the wisest results at which *philosophy* will ever arrive."

Moore lies in Bronham Churchyard, within sight of Sloperton Cottage. In 1948 the Moore Society of Dublin tried to have his body exhumed and reburied in Ireland, but the attempt failed.[13] A hideous statue of him stands in front of Trinity College, staring at the Bank of Ireland.[14] But in Bronham his grave is marked by an Irish cross (erected in 1906) which bears the words: "The poet of all circles and the idol of his own."

Bessy lived alone and neglected in Sloperton Cottage on the £300 pension and £3000 she received from the publishers for her husband's journal and letters. In his will he had asked Lord Russell to edit them. Bessy gave his library to the Royal Irish Academy. A childless widow—she who had been the mother of five and forty-one years a wife—she joined him in death in 1865.

CHAPTER 2

Songs, Set to Music

I "The Bard of Ireland"

IF Thomas Moore is to be remembered at all today, it must be for the poems he wrote to be sung—lyrics fitted to already existing airs. Of these, far and away the most important are the *Irish Melodies.* Up to fifty years ago at least, nearly every English-speaking person, from operatic stars to members of family gatherings around the piano, knew and sang "Believe Me, If All Those Endearing Young Charms," "The Last Rose of Summer," and "The Harp That Once through Tara's Halls." Almost as many were familiar with others—"Oh! Breathe Not His Name!," "She Is Far from the Land," "Go Where Glory Waits Thee," "The Meeting of the Waters," "Dear Harp of My Country," and perhaps, in masculine company, "The Time I've Lost in Wooing."

Our grandfathers would not have needed to be reminded of this: to them Moore *was* the *Irish Melodies.* Just as the more topical of the songs became hymns and political rallying calls in embattled Ireland, soldiers on both sides in the American Civil War, not all of them of Irish descent, sang them together in camp. They were popular songs in the truest sense, and not only in Ireland, England, and the United States. They were translated into the major European languages, including Polish and Russian. Through concerts and reprints they spread over the civilized globe. In America, they were pirated early; in 1816, when only six of the eventual ten volumes had appeared in London or Dublin, there was a pirated Philadelphia edition. Moore was delighted by this news, Federalist Philadelphia of that era being to him "the only place I have seen in the United States which I have one wish to pause in." (Literary piracy was no crime at this time, English works being not yet protected by copyright in America. International copyright did not become law in this country until 1891.)

Moore took such publication as being flattering evidence of his fame; other authors, notably Dickens, decidedly did not.)

(The *Irish Melodies* are then in some sense Moore's greatest and perhaps only claim to lasting distinction. And yet these songs, world-famous in their day, were literally written to order—just as Burns wrote poems to traditional Scottish airs. In 1782, Dr. James McDonnell called together a gathering of the traditional Irish harpers—what was left of them, mostly very old men—just as in more recent times collectors have transcribed and recorded the folk songs of the Appalachian mountaineers. In those days before electrical tape-recording, all McDonnell could do was write down the tunes as he heard them. They interested musicologists, and from 1790 on, various volumes came out incorporating some of these airs, set to words by numerous versifiers.) None of these volumes was in Gaelic, nor was any serious pretense made that the verses were translations from the Gaelic. The harpers themselves may well have known no words for most of the songs.

(The best known of these books was Edward Bunting's *General Collection of the Ancient Irish Melodies*, published in 1796. Edward Hudson, Moore's friend and fellow student in Trinity, knew this collection and brought it to Moore's attention. The budding poet and romantic patriot was fired at once by this enterprise, wrote to Bunting, and asked for an opportunity to contribute to any future volumes. Bunting declined the offer; Moore's name was unknown to him, and he was satisfied with the writers who had served him before. Ironically, when the *Irish Melodies* did appear under another imprint—the airs, of course, were public property—Bunting, gracious if probably chagrined, said generously that they were "the most beautiful popular songs . . . composed by any lyric poet.")

(The Dublin partner of the brother-publishers the Powers, William Power, was also acquainted with Bunting's and other editors' collections; and he was impressed by young Moore's growing local reputation as a poet. He conceived a profitable scheme. He offered Moore an annuity of £500 a year to write lyrics for the traditional tunes, to be issued regularly as a series. He and his brother James, in London, arranged to bring out Irish and English editions jointly, the Dublin edition always to appear first. But London was more important than Dublin as a publishing center,

and gradually James Power (and Moore with him) came to think
of the growing series as his property.

The brothers became alienated, on this and other grounds, and
finally quarreled bitterly. From partners they became inimical rivals. From Volume 8 onward, it was James who published and
William who pirated—with James seeking and securing injunc-
tions against him. In the early days, Sir John Stevenson, who
was Irish, was employed to arrange the tunes; and his arrangements were sometimes not too close to the rough, authentic air.
After the break, James Power handed the music arrangements
over to Henry (later Sir Henry) Rowley Bishop, who is known
today chiefly as composer of the music of "Home, Sweet Home,"
to words by the American, John Howard Payne. Stevenson,
though he took liberties with the old tunes, had an Irishman's feeling for them; Bishop, who was English, had none. All the more
celebrated of the *Irish Melodies, as songs,* were Stevenson's work.
Not only did the music decline after the quarrel, but Moore's
poems also are on the whole inferior in the later volumes to those
in the earlier ones. In part, however, this may be due to simple
fatigue and the dwindling supply of singable tunes.

The salient fact to keep in mind is that the *Irish Melodies* (and
for that matter the *National Airs* and *Sacred Songs* as well) are
words set to music, and must be so regarded. Moore himself said
that all his poetry grew out of his "deep feeling for music." He
was a musician before he was a poet—though he became a better
poet than he ever was a musician. L. A. G. Strong, who called the
Irish Melodies "Moore's title to immortality," pointed out that the
words and music are indivisible, that the songs were written to be
sung.[1] "Only in his best work, in the fittest of the *Irish Melodies,*
which must be considered always with the airs to which they were
written, does he transcend his limitations and reach . . . evoca-
tive power." [2]

Moore himself remarked that he was "better able to vouch for
the sound than for the sense." There were complaints that he had
changed the airs to fit the words; and to a certain extent they are
justified: where it was not Stevenson who "changed the airs,"
Moore was sometimes obliged to do so, to make them singable.
Technically, Moore was a cunning artificer; the vowels and conso-
nants in a line were nicely proportioned, and had to be adjusted

to the exigencies of the music, but sometimes it was more effective to adjust the music to the exigencies of the words.

Knowing no Gaelic, he yet somehow caught the essential Gaelic rhythm, and the Gaelic device of assonance. But harp music transposed to the piano—and Stevenson not only "regularized" the airs but frequently added bravura passages of his own in the fashion current in his times—cannot sound exactly the same. Inevitably it ceases to be folk music and becomes popular music instead. Moore sang these songs himself, many hundreds of times; he was obligated to sing them in company by the terms of his contract. He evolved his own interpretations, suitable to his clear but small tenor. By stressing the vowel sounds, he evolved a style of singing that was almost recitative. He considered this the only proper way in which his songs should be rendered, and he protested any changes made by Power when they were published for others to sing.

John A. Robinson, writing for students of music, sums up this aspect of the *Irish Melodies* when he says: "To be appraised fairly, Moore's lyrics should not be judged apart from the music they were written to accompany. . . . It is a matter for wonder that they stand so highly as poetry apart from the music." [3]

But poetry they are, and must so be considered. Moore recognized the weaknesses in the songs—what he called their "fluidity," probably meaning their overfluency, and their yielding to artificial "conceits." Other critics were harsher than this. Henry Hazlitt attacked them as "prettinesses pass[ing] for patriotism," and said that Moore had converted "the wild harp of Erin into a musical snuff-box." [4] Richard Garnett deprecated their "tricks of diction." [5] A modern author sneers at "the swooning anapests made fashionable by Moore's *Irish Melodies*." [6]

Not lacking also were critics who judged the *Irish Melodies* from a political rather than from a literary standpoint. The Tory press in England thundered that they were "mischievous" and "a vehicle of dangerous politics." They did record the sorrows of oppressed Ireland, and they did celebrate and mourn such leaders as Robert Emmet. This kind of criticism we can discount.

Nevertheless, however factitious they may seem to Gaelic scholars, the *Irish Melodies* breathe the very air of Ireland and speak with Ireland's tones. They made Thomas Moore incontestably "the musical voice of Ireland." The best of them, Strong says truly, are "perfect of their kind, and a kind rare in the English language." [7] Walter Bagehot, the Victorian economist who was also a literary critic, though objecting that the songs "had a little falsetto in them," yet acknowledges them to be "the best of that sort we have"; and Howard Mumford Jones calls them "in their own genre absolutely flawless and absolutely right." [8] We shall examine them more closely in assessing Moore as a lyrist.

II *The Later Song Series*

Besides the *Irish Melodies,* Moore's other song series were *National Airs* and *Sacred Songs.* He wrote many other poems that were intended to be sung or could be and have been set to music (*Evenings in Greece* is an example), and interspersed in the narrative poems are other short lyrics, some of which have been sung oftener than they have been read. But these three were the only ones which came out year after year in a long sequence—there were ten volumes of the *Irish Melodies,* six of the *National Airs,* and two of the *Sacred Songs.*

Unfortunately, as the seemingly endless numbers were published, it became impossible for Moore, prolific as he was, to keep up the verve of the earlier collections. Cumulative boredom crept in. He was a good enough critic of his work to realize that his songs (especially the *Irish Melodies*) were the likeliest of all his writing to survive—he wrote to Longmans, "In a race to future times, . . . those little ponies, the Melodies, will beat the mare Lalla Rookh." Yet to a certain extent the production of song lyrics became an industry, instead of a bubbling from the spring of inspiration. This became increasingly apparent in *National Airs,* and obvious in *Sacred Songs.*

If only the very best of all the songs could have been printed together, and the residue suppressed, we should be better able to appreciate properly their real value. But the songs were Moore's chief means of livelihood for a long time; and besides, he, his publishers, and his immediate public were all too kind and too undiscriminating to have permitted any such radical editing.

This evaluation of his work becomes most relevant when we read today the *National Airs.* Supposedly these were lyrics set to anonymous tunes, allegedly folk songs from more than a dozen nations and provinces. Some of these ascriptions seem certainly apocryphal; none of the airs was well-known. Perhaps the only one of the *National Airs* that is even faintly familiar today is "Oft, in the Stilly Night," set to "a Scotch air." (This is the only kind of provenance given to any them.)

For the most part, though some of the *National Airs* display more energy than do the more languorous of the *Irish Melodies,* they are notable for Moore's unfailing craftsmanship more than for beauty. Few of them can stand as poems in their own right, and they echo the sentimentality of too many of his lyrics. The music to which they were set was "arranged" by Bishop, whose characteristic ornamentation destroys any folk quality of the tunes—a quality which in Stevenson, for all his "improvements," was never completely hidden.

The *Sacred Songs* were intended to be, and often actually were, sung as hymns in church. Although several are set to tunes from Haydn (the only well-known composer represented), none of Moore's lyrics has the vigor and grandeur of, say, Addison's "The Spacious Firmament on High," set to Haydn's music. None of them can be thought of as an orthodox Christian hymn. They are notable chiefly as expressions of Moore's vague romantic religious feeling:

> The turf shall be my fragrant shrine;
> My temple, Lord! that Arch of thine;
> My censer's breath the mountain airs,
> And silent thoughts my only prayers!

This is almost pantheism. Not one of Moore's hymns is included in the most comprehensive modern hymnals. If any of them survives at all, it may be "Sound the Loud Timbrel," which was occasionally sung in Sunday schools early in this century.

As Strong says, "the *Sacred Songs* might have been written by anybody." [9]

III   *Moore as a Song Writer*

Anyone conditioned to contemporary poetry—or even to magazine verse—who reads the *Irish Melodies* for the first time today may well be repelled (or worse, bored) by their sentimentality, too often verging on the maudlin; their artificial conceits; their "thees" and "thous"; and their sometimes singsong rhythm.

But look a little deeper. Moore, if one observes him well, is "always the artist, not the clumsy craftsman." [10] This is not altogether a collection of "swooning anapests." Moore was a master verse technician, capable, when the music permitted, of daring experimentation in meter. Proof of this assertion becomes evident when one reads aloud, for example, "At the Mid Hour of Night":

At the mid hour of night, when stars are weeping, I fly
To the lone vale we loved, when life shone warm in thine eye;
And I think oft, if spirits can steal from the region of air,
To revisit past scenes of delight, thou wilt come to me there,
And tell me our love is remember'd, even in the sky.

Moore is always in control, and his technique is not only metrically interesting but a successful effort to avoid monotony. Despite all contemporary criteria, it is also genuine poetry.
There are other instances as in "Drink of This Cup":

Would you forget the dark world we are in,
Just taste of the bubble that gleams on the top of it;
But would you rise above earth, till akin
To Immortals themselves, you must drain every drop of it.

Or from "The Irish Peasant to His Mistress":

Through grief and through danger thy smile hath cheer'd my
way,
Till hope seemed to bud from each thorn that round me lay;
The darker our fortune, the brighter our pure love burn'd,
Till shame into glory, till fear into zeal was turn'd;
Yes, slave as I was, in thy arms my spirit felt free,
And bless'd even the sorrows that made me more dear to thee.

Sometimes it is merely good rousing verse, as in "When the Wine-Cup Is Smiling," from *National Airs* (otherwise unascribed quotations are from the *Irish Melodies*): "When the wine-cup is smiling before us,/And we pledge round to hearts that are true, boy, true"; or "They May Rail at This Life":

> They may rail at this life—from the hour I began it,
> I found it a life of kindness and bliss;
> And until they can show me some happier planet,
> More social and bright, I'll content me with this.

But Scott or Longfellow as balladist could well have written "Peace to the Slumb'rer" (from *National Airs*):

> Peace to the slumb'rers!
> They lie on the battle-plain,
> With no shroud to cover them;
> The dew and the summer rain
> Are all that weep over them.

And if there is a hint of Poe in "I Would I Were by That Dim Lake," then the echo, if echo it be, comes from his American admirer to the older poet.

> The lifeless sky, the mournful sound
> Of unseen waters falling round;
> The dry leaves quiv'ring o'er my head,
> Like man, unquiet ev'n when dead!
> These, ay, these shall wean
> My soul from life's deluding scene,
> And turn each thought, o'ercharged with gloom,
> Like willows, downwards tow'rds the tomb—

True, Moore is not of the company of the great. One accidental coincidence may show the difference between high talent and technical competence, and towering genius. Here is Moore:

> As a beam o'er the face of the waters may glow
> While the tide runs in darkness and coldness below,
> So the cheek may be ting'd with a warm sunny smile,
> Though the cold heart to ruin runs darkly the while.

And Shelley writes, with approximately the same comparison, in *Adonais*:

[40]

> On the withering flower
> The killing sun shines brightly: on a cheek
> The life may burn in blood, even while the heart may break.

The obvious gulf is enormous.

Yet even a minor poet may produce a few great poems. Moore
can transcend himself; the facile singer can become for a moment
the vatic bard. Would anyone expect that the author of "Erin!
the Tear and the Smile in Thine Eyes" or "Oh! Had We Some
Bright Little Isle of Our Own" could also be the author of the
magnificent and haunting "Oh, Ye Dead"?—

> "Oh, ye Dead! Oh, ye Dead! whom we know by the light you
> give
> From your cold gleaming eyes, though you move like men
> who live,
> Why leave you thus your graves,
> In far off fields and waves,
> Where the worm and the sea-bird only know your bed,
> To haunt this spot where all
> Those eyes that wept your fall,
> And the hearts that wailed you, like your own, lie dead?"

The answer, perhaps, is that Moore cannot hold to his highest
achievement: the truly great poet can. The second stanza is quite
inferior to the first. Nevertheless, it is easy to understand why Stephen Gwynn, in contradiction to the usual judgment, called
Moore "a poet first, a musician afterward," [11] or why Mary Shelley
wrote to Moore: "The department of poetry peculiarly your own
[is] songs instinct with the intense principle of life and love." But
Moore the lyrist aspired also to be Moore the poetic narrator. He
must be judged in both capacities.

CHAPTER 3

Poems That Tell a Story

I Lalla Rookh

A FEW of Moore's lyrics have earned a modest immortality, and are thereby for all time. *Lalla Rookh* was strictly for the time in which it was written. Reading it today is a task, not a pleasure. It is long, drawn-out, florid, bathetic, and occasionally absurd.

Yet there are alleviations—felicitous phrases, lively fancy, vigorous if melodramatic moments in the two better of the four episodes, and most particularly in the prose interludes, which reveal the keen ironic wit always underlying Moore's artificial sentimentality. If we are brought up short by such nonsense as "Though Reason's self be wreck'd,/Safe 'mid the ruins of her intellect," or "Nor could her mind, whose beam/As yet was weak, penetrate half his scheme." yet there are "The punctual sounds/Of the small drums with which they count the night"—rousing rhythms and apt words. There are also pleasant if vague descriptions of imaginary semi-Oriental landscapes—even though Moore is always weak in visual perception.

The long narrative poem is divided into four stories in verse, supposed to be sung by a young minstrel who has joined the wedding party of Lalla Rookh, the beautiful daughter of the Mogul Emperor Aurunzebe (Auranzeb) of India, who with her ladies, officials, and attendants is journeying from Delhi to Cashmere (Kashmir) to marry Akiris, the young king of Bucharia (Bukhara, now a part of the U.S.S.R.), whom she has never seen. The time—though anachronisms abound—seems to be the sixteenth century. Though all concerned are Indian, Moore seems often to equate them with Persians.

Chief of the officials is Fadladeen, Keeper of the Harem, a pedant, a sour critic, and a time-server, who is the butt of Moore's satire throughout the poem. The young minstrel, Feramorz, says on his arrival that he has been sent by the princely bridegroom to accompany the princess and to entertain her and her train during the long journey. The two fall in love, and Lalla Rookh, who has hitherto been acquiescent to her marriage, is in despair as she endeavors in vain to suppress her feeling for Feramorz. At last they reach Kashmir, and there she learns, more to her surprise than the reader's, that the minstrel was the king himself in disguise.

The four stories recited or sung by Feramorz are "The Veiled Prophet of Khorassan" (Khorasan, Iran), "Paradise and the Peri," "The Fire-Worshippers," and "The Light of the Haram" (as Moore always spells "harem"). All are vaguely Indian or Persian in setting. Actually Moore had no previous knowledge of or special interest in the Near East. He was following the fashion of his day, the passion for the Oriental, which after Napoleon's campaign in Egypt and British incursions into India had seized the imagination of the English. The motto of popular poetry was "Stick to the East." Byron's *Bride of Abydos* and *The Giaour* had appeared in 1813 and *The Corsair* (which he had offered to withdraw when he learned that Moore also was mining the Oriental vein) in 1814. The Orient, in a word, was all the rage, and Moore took the theme as a deliberate assignment. He boned for it in Lord Lansdowne's library, and delivered his findings in the form of copious footnotes. Howard Mumford Jones spoke truly when he said that "Moore's perfumed Orient discovers always a lurking odor of old leather bindings." [1]

Today such a work would probably be a collection of novellas in prose. In 1817 "everybody" read narrative verse instead. In two of the stories Moore's own mind and heart became engaged, and they are by far the best. In two of them he was merely catering to the popular taste. The weak two are "Paradise and the Peri" and "The Light of the Haram." In the former, a female peri is told by the angel guarding the gate of Paradise

> The Peri yet may be forgiven
> Who brings to this Eternal gate
> The Gift that is most dear to Heav'n.

(A peri is a Persian fairy, descended from the union of a fallen angel with a mortal, and thus by "the sins of the fathers" excluded from Paradise.)

She finds and offers successively the last drop of blood from the heart of a youthful warrior killed in battle with a tyrant, and the sigh of a maiden for her dead lover. (Fadladeen remarks later that these, and particularly the sigh, would be a bit difficult to transport!) Both are rejected by the angelic sentry. Then she gathers and presents the tear of a repentant sinner—and that earns her entry into Paradise. What Moore himself thought of this sugary romance may be gathered from the caustic comments of Fadladeen. "The Light of the Haram" is still slighter and more saccharine. It narrates only a quarrel and reconciliation between Emperor Selim and his favorite wife, Nourmahal.

But with "The Veiled Prophet of Khorassan" we come to a more robust theme. Moore hated demagoguery as much as he hated oppression—it was the cause of his long dissension with Daniel O'Connell, the chief Irish leader of the time—and in this poem he gives his hatred full vent. It is the story of a demagogue who is also a hypocrite, a lecher, a tyrant, and a murderer.

Mokanna, the prophet, wears a silver veil which is supposed to hide his glory of countenance from his followers, who could not have endured its radiance: it hides in fact a hideous and evil face. He has bound to him, by an unholy oath forced upon her in a charnel house, the lovely young Zelica, whose mind has become deranged by grief for her lover Azim, reported to have been killed in the Persian war in Thrace. The announcement of Azim's death was false, and he reappears, this time as leader of a rebellion against Mokanna. He is horrified to discover Zelica, the chaste maiden he loves, apparently the paramour of the prophet. Mokanna and his troops are near defeat, and in a frenzy he calls his disciples to a banquet, brazenly admits his true nature and purpose, casts off the veil to show them his real visage—and poisons them all, taunting them as they die. He battles on alone, compelling Zelica to stand by him. As he falls, he throws the silver veil over her, and Azim, taking her for the prophet, kills her. Azim spends the remainder of his life praying beside her tomb.

This theme of revolt against tyranny caught hold of Moore—almost as in *The Revolt of Islam* it caught hold of the young Shelley

—and it carried him to rhetorical but noble passages typical of the Romantic poets, and far removed from his trite and improbable story.

> When the glad Slave shall at these feet let down
> His broken chain, the tyrant Lord his crown,
> The Priest his book, the Conqueror his wreath,
> And from the lips of Truth one mighty breath
> Shall like a whirlwind, scatter in its breeze
> That whole dark pile of human mockeries,
> Then shall the reign of Mind commence on earth,
> And starting fresh as from a second birth,
> Man, in the sunshine of the world's new spring,
> Shall walk transparent like some holy thing!

These words, reminiscent of Rousseau or William Godwin, are put in the mouth of the lying prophet Mokanna. Yet they are the very voice of the Enlightenment that came in the wake of the French Revolution—that era when, in Wordsworth's phrase, "bliss was it in that dawn to be alive." [2] To Moore they might appropriately be spoken by a rabble rouser—but even against his will he too was affected by that perfectionist dream. That the dream was often worded in bombast is less a reflection on him or any other of the Romantics than a blemish on the literary taste of the age.

That Moore could express himself in strong and exalted verse as well as in languor and sweetness is also evident throughout "The Veiled Prophet of Khorassan."

> As a grim tiger, whom the torrent's might
> Surprises in some parched ravine at night,
> Turns, ev'n in drowning, on the wretched flocks
> Swept with him in that snow-flood from the rocks,
> And, to the last, devouring on his way,
> Bloodies the stream he hath not power to stay—

thus he describes Mokanna's slaughter of his defeated followers. Again, witness the powerful scene in which the prophet bids a mocking farewell to the disciples he has murdered: "There, ye wise Saints, behold your Light, your Star—/Ye *would* be dupes and victims, and ye *are*." It is rank melodrama; but it *moves*.

Best of all the parts of *Lalla Rookh* is "The Fire Worshippers." Ostensibly it is an account of the struggle of the persecuted Persian Ghebers (Parsees) against their Moslem oppressors. Obviously Moore has identified the Ghebers with the persecuted Irish struggling against England. In Hafed, the young leader of the rebellion, there is more than a hint of Robert Emmet.

There is a slight love story in this poem—a "Romeo and Juliet" theme, with Hafed as Romeo and Hinda, daughter of the Moslem Emir, as Juliet. She has fallen in love with Hafed without knowing that he is one of the hated fire-worshipers; when she learns the truth it is too late to steel her heart against him. Hafed, beaten, makes his way to the fire tower and dies in the holy flame; whereupon Hinda drowns herself.

What gives life and power to this poem, however, is the revolt of the Zoroastrians against their Arab conquerors. In the end Hafed becomes almost a mask for Emmet; and it is the fury of the "born" Irish rebel in Moore, not the moderation of the Anglophile semi-Whig, that describes in blazing scorn

> One of that saintly, murd'rous brood,
> To carnage and the Koran giv'n,
> Who think through unbelievers' blood
> Lies their directed path to heav'n.

Characteristically, it is not Mohammedanism or any other religion that in itself arouses Moore's ire; it is that aberration of religion called fanaticism:

> Just Alla[h]! what must be thy look,
> When such a wretch before thee stands
> Unblushing, with thy Sacred Book,—
> Turning the leaves with blood-stained hands,
> And wresting from its page sublime
> His creed of lust, and hate, and crime?

Thus the Moore who was so complaisant to the Church of England never forgave the Church of Ireland for its oppression of and bigoted zeal against the Irish Catholics. It is no wonder that Fadladeen condemns this as "a profane and seditious story"!

Unhappily when one gathers gems from *Lalla Rookh*, one can

do so only by wading through vast stretches of scented mud. It is Hinda who "ever thus, from childhood's hour" had "seen my fondest hopes decay," and it is over her watery grave that the peris sing: "Farewell—be it ours to embellish thy pillow/With ev'rything beauteous that grows in the deep." The thought of Hinda's pillow being embellished with starfish and sea urchins is arresting.

Again a concidence of subject provides a useful lesson in the difference between talent and genius. At Selim's feast, in "The Light of the Haram,"

> The board was spread with fruits and wine;
> With grapes of gold, like those that shine
> On Casbin's hills;—pomegranates full
> Of melting sweetness, and the pears
> And sunniest apples that Cambul
> In all its thousand gardens bears—

and so on. Compare this passage with that magic one in Keats's *Eve of St. Agnes* where Porphyro set out for Madeline in her bedchamber

> Jellies soother than the creamy curd,
> And lucent syrups, tinct with cinnamon;
> Manna and dates, in argosy transferr'd
> From Fez; and spicèd dainties, every one,
> From silken Samarcand to cedar'd Lebanon.

Keats needs no explanatory footnotes; Moore gives them plenteously, annotating each allusion, to prove the labor they cost him. He knew that himself, and said that he hoped to make up for any deficiencies in the poem by "versatility and polish." He spoke of *Lalla Rookh* as "something, I hope, that will place me above the vulgar herd both of worldlings and critics." He had been stung by his dismissal as a light erotic versifier. But it is not thus that one regards inspired poems. There is always about Moore a touch of the bookish, the instructive, the edifying.

In a word, *Lalla Rookh* was written to make money and win reputation, an honest enough aim for a professional writer such as Moore was. He was already in a position where he knew publishers would compete for him. When word got around that he was writing a long poem on the fashionable Orient, John Murray offered him two thousand guineas for it. His own publishers, Longmans, to whom he had gone as soon as returns had wiped out his indebtedness to his early Irish publisher, James Carpenter, thereupon countered with a proffer of three thousand guineas—and even offered to accept the poem before reading it! It finally appeared under the Longmans imprint in May of 1817; the second edition came out in June, the third in July, and there were countless others.

In the midst of the public delirium—as Jones says, "*Lalla Rookh* was the culminating point in poetical Orientalism." [3] — there were dissident notes; and they were not all from politically activated critics. The more acute readers were quick to pounce upon its weaknesses. Leigh Hunt called it "too florid," and deplored Moore's writing about places and people of which he had no first-hand knowledge. Later critics have all agreed with L. A. G. Strong that "compared with the other second-, third-, and fourth-rate work of the period it is well enough." Of it, he adds, "the less said the better." [4] George Saintsbury ridiculed the "parade of second- or third- or twentieth-hand learning in the notes." Yet he was compelled to concede that to Moore's contemporaries he was "the author of this poem chiefly," and that to him "it still seems a very remarkable poem of the second rank." [5] Stephen Gwynn echoes Saintsbury: "A work of very secondary merit" which "retains its place in literature mainly as an example of an extinct taste." [6] And Howard Mumford Jones pretty well sums it up by saying that "it lies stranded in the Dead Sea of literature, and few there are who climb aboard and explore its faded interior." [7]

Yet dull and artificial as *Lalla Rookh* often is, it still has some interest for the student of poetic technique. There are far too many monotonous couplets in iambic pentameter and of iambic tetrameter stanzas in an a-b-a-b-c-c-d-e-f-e-f rhyme-scheme. On the other hand, there is sometimes a bold manipulation of dactyls and anapests that lifts the lush verse above its usual self and strikes a note of true music. In this metric form, later to be used with so much distinction by Shelley, Moore was a pioneer. As Gwynn points out, he was the first to use it "with dexterity and confidence." [8]

II   The Loves of the Angels

Moore's other major narrative poem is *The Loves of the Angels,* which is much shorter than *Lalla Rookh.* As was noted previously, this poem originally dealt with the confessions by three fallen angels of their love affairs with mortal women, which caused their expulsion from the orthodox Christian heaven. This caused such a clamor from the devout that from the fifth edition on, Moore revamped the stories and made the angels Mohammedan seraphs expelled from the Moslem Paradise.

Of course all of pagan mythology is full of such unions between gods and human beings: Zeus, among his other attributes, was a great womanizer; and Apollo was not far behind him. Almost every religion includes similar stories in its canon; the peris, as we have seen, were the offspring of angels and mortals, and it is a myth common to both Islam and Christianity. It should have occurred to the protesters that, according to Genesis 6:2, "the sons of God [Hebrew *elohim,* a plural] saw the daughters of men that they were fair; and they took them wives of all that they chose." The net result of Moore's yielding to pressure was more of his customary footnotes, thus adding to the bookishness of the poem.

The first angel, who is unnamed, fell captive to the wiles of a girl named Lea, whose only interest in him was to find a way by which she herself could get into heaven.

> She loved me, but as one of race
> Angelic, . . .
>   Wishing for wings that she might go
> Out of this shadowy world below
> To that free, glorious element.

In return for only a kiss on her brow, she persuaded him to recite the spell "that plumes my wings for heaven." (Regrettably, she plied him with wine to weaken his resistance, which is distinctly against Mohammedan tenets.) As soon as he uttered the spell, she seized advantage of it and flew upwards out of his sight forever; when he sought to follow, the magic had lost its power, and he was doomed to a lonely mundane existence through eternity.

Rubi, the second angel, was endowed with a thirst for knowledge that had set him circling all the planets until, with the crea-

tion of woman on Earth, his "wish to know" became concentrated
on this entrancing new creature; he was enthralled not by her
beauty alone but by "the mind outshining clear/Through the
whole frame." Rather oddly, even after Rubi has become an Is-
lamic angel, it is Eve and the Garden of Eden that he describes.
Eve was not for him; instead, he found and fell in love with Lilis,
who unfortunately possessed as much curiosity as he. As Psyche
with Cupid, she badgered him to display himself just once in all
his celestial glory. To his sorrow he yielded at last, but the instant
he touched her she burst into flame. She branded him with her
dying kiss, and now he roams the earth beseeching heaven to par-
don her and punish him instead: "To save one minute's pain to
her/Let mine last all eternity!"

Zaraph, the third angel, has the most commonplace and domes-
tic story and affords the dullest verse. He fell in love with Nama:
"The love for the Creator soon/In passion for the creature ended."
They were married, which ended any possibility of his ever returning to Paradise. But heaven was merciful to this mild couple,
giving them as "their only punishment/(As wrong, however
sweet, must bear its brand)" the decree that "they both shall wan-
der here . . . throughout all time," pilgrims forever pursuing
"their pathway towards eternity."

The whole poem is vaguely allegorical, semierotic, full of a
rather dreamy religiosity. Moore said that it had been turned into
verse from an earlier prose narrative which, if it ever existed, has
not survived. Its melody is monotonous—iambic pentameter or
tetrameter, in couplets or in an a-b-a-b- rhyme-scheme, without
any of the arresting metrical variations that elevate *Lalla Rookh*.
Its imagery is shifting and indefinite. It descends to such bathos
as

> The glory of young womankind
> Taken, in their perfection, warm,
> Ere time had chilled a single charm,

or "Oh Love, Religion, Music, all/That's left of Eden upon Earth."

It does, however, since "Melody Moore" wrote it, have its musical moments to relieve the generally dreary accounts of "that hour
unblest" when each of the fallen seraphs "for Woman's smile . . .

lost the skies." It even has a few phrases of pure poetry—e.g., "She moved in light of her own making." Its very beginning has a springlike, almost Chaucerian ring:

> 'Twas when the world was in its prime,
> When the fresh stars had just begun
> Their race of glory, and young Time
> Told his first birth-days by the sun.

The poem, one regrets to say, does not sustain this level.

Understandably, *The Loves of the Angels* even in its own time never enjoyed the sensational popularity of *Lalla Rookh*. Moore felt keenly the attacks on it as irreligious and erotic. It certainly is not irreligious; and its strained sentimentality is far from erotic in any proper sense; it hints at "passion" and "desire," but it never displays them. Moore confided sadly to his journal that "what I thought the best, as well as the most moral thing I had ever written" was condemned as "improper." But, he heartened himself by reflecting, Lord Lansdowne "thought the poem not only beautiful but perfectly unexceptionable and pure."

One contemporary critic called it "disgusting nonsense," though he added that "as far as melody and imagery are its essentials, its beauty can hardly farther go" [9]—a verdict which cannot be echoed, in either judgment, by later readers: much of it is nonsense, but it is not disgusting. Neither would they echo William Jerdan, who ascribed to it "sparkling brilliancy and breathing beauty." [10] But Jerdan himself was constrained to add a condemnation of its "fictitious sentiment" and "the ingenious trifling of fanciful conceit."

The Loves of the Angels has had its admirers, though Stephen Gwynn seems to be the only one who sets it above *Lalla Rookh*. Its mixed reception may have convinced Moore that narrative verse was not his *metier*, if *Alciphron* was written earlier, as seems likely, *The Loves of the Angels* may have been his swan-song so far as serious poetry is concerned.

III Alciphron

Alciphron is Moore's only other attempt to tell a serious story in verse. (There is a story of sorts in *The Fudge Family in England*,

but it is purely humorous and satirical.) *Alciphron* is only a frag-
ment, an unfinished poetic version of his only prose tale, *The Epicurean*. It appears to have been written before *The Epicurean*,
and probably was cut short because Moore realized that it would
read better in prose. What there is of it is told in a series of letters,
from Alciphron in Egypt to his friend Cleon in Athens, followed
by one from the Egyptian priest Orcus to the (Roman?) pretorian
prefect, Decius. The story, such as it is, deals with a young Greek
philosopher who travels to Egypt in search of religious truth.

Moore's numerous historical and theological anachronisms
make the poem difficult to understand, even as to the time in
which it is supposed to be set. It is a mishmash of Christianity,
Gnosticism, Platonism, and the ancient Egyptian religion. Moore
seems to have known as little about Greece (except for its classic
literature) as he knew about Egypt. One howler is irresistible:
with a sublime ignorance of the almost Oriental position of
women in Greece up to modern times, he depicts "some fair Athe-
nian maid" sitting on the marble steps,

> Over some favorite volume bending;
> And by her side a youthful sage
> Holds back the ringlets that descending
> Would close o'ershadow all the page.

Respectable ancient Greek women stayed at home in their own
quarters, and they were illiterate; no "sage," youthful or otherwise, would have cooperated in such an indecent display!

Alciphron does evidence Moore's lifelong interest in theological
speculation, most decisively expressed in the prose *Travels of an
Irish Gentleman in Search of a Religion,* which, though published
before *Alciphron,* was written much later. *Alciphron* reveals also
the abiding anticlericalism, perhaps caught in childhood from his
father:

> None of all our creedless school
> E'er conned, believed, or reverenced less
> The fables of the priest-led fool
> Who tells us of a soul, a mind,
> Separate and pure within us shrined.

This sounds almost like Rationalism, but Moore writes it to refute it; he was always at the very least a Deist.

Considered solely as poetry, *Alciphron* is talky and exceedingly dull. It is written in the accustomed iambic tetrameters or pentameters, with their sleep-inducing monotony. Moore's usual sure touch in the singability of verse falters badly: how, for example, could a born musician ever have passed so incredibly bad a line as "How lovelily they all must shine"?

Yet even this patent failure of a poem has its alleviating moments. There are striking images, such as of the pyramids "standing sublime/'Twixt earth and heaven, the watch-towers of Time"; or of the Egyptian dead who

> Lie in their painted coverings,
> And on each new successor race
> That visit their dim haunts below
> Look with the same unwithering face
> They wore three thousand years ago—

though one would hardly think of a mummy as "unwithering." There is also a fine description of the City of the Dead, in Memphis, where

> Pyramid over pyramid
> Tower in succession to the skies;
> While one, aspiring, as if soon
> 'T would touch the heavens, rose over all,
> And on its summit, the white moon
> Rested as on a pedestal!

(This also contains one of the few relieving exceptions in *Alciphron* to the monotonous regularity of the meter.)

But Moore undoubtedly came to understand that narrative poetry was not his forte. In so far as he was an authentic poet, he was a singer of songs. *Lalla Rookh* had been written almost to order; *The Loves of the Angels* was patently an attempt to follow up that tremendous success; and *Alciphron*, it must have been obvious from the first, was a foreordained failure. So far as is known, he never contemplated again the production of a long narrative poem.

He did, however, write an enormous amount of other verse. As the years went on, that portion of his literary career which antedated his absorption in biography and history may be divided roughly into overlapping and interlocking periods. First he was "Anacreon Moore," then "Melody Moore"; then, so to speak, he became "Lalla Rookh Moore," and then "Political Satire Moore." It is in this last capacity that Moore's verse must next be considered.

CHAPTER 4

Verse Satire and Polemics

I *The Topical Versifier*

IT IS doubtful if Moore ever understood entirely the exact nature of his talent. His enormous popularity justified him in his own mind as an aspirant to the first rank of English poetry: he had heard himself acclaimed often enough as the supreme English poet of his day. He knew in his more objective moments that he had not attained that rank and never could attain it. Still, he was apt to deprecate the very things that he could do better than any of his contemporaries—light, sentimental poems to be sung, and pungent irony and satire in verse. With the latter—though he was likely to slip from indignation into bombast—may be included his angry, nonsatiric polemic poems.

As time went on and weariness grew within him, the poetic spring dried and he turned more and more to topical verse. What he never lost was his technical expertise. The least of his squibs for *The Times* and *The Morning Chronicle* displayed to the end his old polish and sting. If so much of his satirical verse is no longer readable, it is not because of the writing but because the objects of his ridicule and wrath have faded into the shadows of old political history, which nobody but professional historians would care to grope about in today.

To the first reader who came upon it in his morning paper, or ink-fresh in a slender pamphlet, it was immediate, exhilarating, and (if he were a Tory, or an admirer of the Regent) maddening. Basically Moore's wit exploded in harmless fireworks and his humor was kindly; but when it came to the Irish cause or to one or two other subjects it could turn savage and the fireworks stung. Some of his attacks on the Established Church of Ireland were so vicious that he himself excluded them from his collected poems. Moore, who hated few things and few people, never lost his hatred for the Church which extracted tithes from starving Irish peasants to whom its tenets were rank heresy; or for Lord Castlereagh, who (himself Anglo-Irish) had, as a chief secretary, suppressed the United Irishmen's revolt in 1798, and who, until his suicide in 1822, was the leader and voice of the most extreme reaction at home and abroad. On these two subjects Moore could be and was venomous.

The Prince of Wales, whom as Regent Moore had believed in and flattered, had gone back on all his liberal promises when he succeeded as George IV. Eventually, Moore came to regard him as a figure of fun, rather than as an object of indignation. Other things—slavery, child labor, corruption, religious bigotry—could arouse him to anger; but most of his satirical poems display contempt rather than fury. He was a master of irony as well as of more obvious satire; and irony, though it may well be cutting, is seldom as heated as is the open lampoon.

Whatever other and different kinds of writing engaged his main attention, Moore continued to write satirical squibs and poems, prolifically up to Catholic Emancipation (1829), more sparingly up to passage of the Reform Bill (1832), and occasionally after that. But with the weakening of his political interests, and his increasing preoccupation with biography and history, his facility fell off. His later satires are labored, and lack the bite of the earlier ones.

II The American Poems

Moore's first verse satire—or, with greater accuracy, his first verse polemic—was the least worthy of him. It was the antidemocratic verse inspired by his visit to the United States of America in 1803. It must be remembered that Moore, however liberal in some of his views, was always against demagoguery and rabblerousing; and that his most cherished associations, at the beginning of his literary career, were with his noble patrons, who may have been enlightened in their opinions but were also fastidious aristocrats. Moore's first noble Whig friend, Lord Moira, had fought against the rebellious colonials in America; his earlier friend, Joseph Atkinson, had served under Moira.

Furthermore Moore was not made for rough provincial society. He was urban as well as urbane. He liked nothing in America except the nearest approximation it could offer to the English circles so dear to him—the well-mannered ladies and gentlemen, mostly of Federalist persuasion, whom he met particularly in Philadelphia. It was the orthodox reaction of British observers for fifty years to come. In the years when Moore could still hail the egregious Regent as "the bright future star of England's throne," he could also indict American society as he saw it as "The apathy of wrong, the bosom's ice,/The slow and cold stagnation into vice." And he could express his anti-Jacobin distaste for "That Gallic garbage of philosophy,/That nauseous slaver of these frantic times."

America to him was the place "Where every ill the ancient world could brew/Is mixt with every grossness of the new." Some of his bias, it is true, arose from his detestation of chattel slavery. In "To the Lord Viscount Forbes" he denounced a land "where bastard Freedom waves/Her fustian flag in mockery o'er slaves." Yet much of it must be credited (or debited) to his shrinking from the uncultured provincialism of rural and small town America in 1803. Later, when he had found subjects more worthy of his blade, he became ashamed of these youthful excesses, and apologized manfully for them.

As a matter of fact, most Americans knew nothing about them. They sang the *Irish Melodies,* and wept over *Lalla Rookh,* and were blissfully ignorant of the disgust and bitterness with which young Thomas Moore had greeted their country on his only visit to its shores.

III *The Polemicist*

Moore learned in time the advantage of ridicule over denunciation. It left its victims helpless except to sputter back. They dared not risk becoming the laughing-stock of all England by imprisoning the most popular poet in the country, as they could imprison a mere impudent journalist or an impoverished printer. However, the earlier long satirical poems (as contrasted with short squibs or pasquinades) were polemic rather than satiric: they did not make fun; they struck out.

In this field Moore made rather an inauspicious beginning. *Corruption, Intolerance,* and *The Sceptic* were planned as the first of a considerable series; but Moore abandoned the scheme when they failed to arouse much interest. He had thought of them as "the imperfect beginning of a long series of [verse] essays addressed to an Englishman by an Irishman," and the frank model was Pope's *Essay on Man* and *Essay on Criticism*. It was a clumsy device, and Moore lacked the staggering, wicked brilliance of Pope. The primary butt of *Corruption* was bribery in high places, but it fanned out to include attacks on both Tory reaction and demagoguery—always Moore's two *bêtes noires*. *Intolerance* applied the whip to bigotry and religious fanaticism. *The Sceptic*, which is subtitled "A Philosophical Satire," is the weakest of the three. None of them is of great importance. A few excerpts will show their flavor.

In *Corruption*, Moore the Irishman voiced his scorn for England the Oppressor. (Moore the Anglophile was in abeyance.)

> I coldly listen to thy patriot vaunts,
> And feel, tho' close our wedded countries twine,
> More sorrow for my own than pride in thine!

He could not forget or forgive the wrongs done his native land: "The dupéd people, hourly doomed to pay/The sums that bribe their liberties away." He ends with an admonition, heartfelt but singularly unprophetic (England being then at the beginning of its greatest age): "Oh England, sinking England! boast no more."

The Muse grows livelier in *Intolerance:* "When bigot zeal her drunken antics plays,/Bigots alike in Rome or England born"— And he condemns equally all religious intolerance, whatever creed may be its spokesman or its victim:

> Yes,—rather plunge me back in Pagan night,
> And take my chance with Socrates for bliss
> Than be the Christian of a faith like this.

There speaks the son of the tolerant, anticlerical John Moore. And the same latitudinarianism emerges from *The Sceptic:* "As who is wise?—you'll find the self-same man/A sage in France, a madman in Japan."

IV *The Edge of the Sword*

With *Intercepted Letters, or the Two-Penny Post-Bag*, Moore found his satirical stride. The "letters" were immensely popular (among, of course, those who agreed with their political views); and they deserved to be. They were supposed to be private letters (though in verse) exchanged by Tory notables, and intercepted, presumably, by the pseudonymous "Thomas Brown the Younger," and they parodied the public style of their alleged authors.[1] The volume carried in its fifth edition a preface by "a friend of the author"—the author being ostensibly "Brown" and the friend very plainly Moore: by this time it was a secret to few.

Many of the "letters" were parodies on popular poems of the time and some of them were parodies on songs and meant to be— and were—sung to the same tune. They are intensely topical, and to read them today with understanding would require a whole volume of explication. Yet they are neatly turned and sharply pointed, and some of them are still very amusing—good journalism rather than poetry in any serious sense.

For the most part, the "letters" were aimed at the Regent, the Tories, and the enemies of Ireland. A few, however, were more general in application, without political significance. The letter from a publisher to an author who has submitted a manuscript would arouse a sympathetic throb in the heart of any writer a century and a half later:

> Per Post, Sir, we send your MS. . . .
> Very sorry, but can't undertake. . . .
> Clever work, Sir! . . .
> Its only defect is—it never would sell.

But the more typical "intercepted letter" makes bitter fun of the fat Regent and his penchant for equally fat and elderly mistresses:

> So, let your list of *she*-promotions
> Include those only, plump and sage,
> Who've reached the *regulation* age;
> That is (as near as one can fix
> From Peerage dates) full fifty-six.

The eight *Fables for the Holy Alliance*[2] were, said Moore, designed to illustrate and make understandable that indefinite and rather mystical declaration. Each Fable is preceded by a Proem

which explains its factual basis. The Fables themselves have sparkle and gaiety; but with no direct involvement with the Irish
question, Moore's habitual good humor overcame him, and they
lack sting. Occasionally he makes his point sharply, as in "The Fly
and the Bullock," where a common household fly occupies the
dais and a bullock the sacrificial altar: "The Fly on the Shrine is
Legitimate Right,/And that Bullock, the People that's sacrificed to
it."

In the Proems Moore's indignation comes out more clearly than
in the Fables themselves. He bursts out in "Church and State"
with

> Religion, made,
> 'Twixt Church and State, a truck, a trade, . . .
> 'Twixt Cant and Blasphemy, the two
> Rank ills with which this age is curst,

or, in "The Extinguishers," remarks sardonically:

> Even soldiers sometimes *think*—
> Nay, Colonels have been known to *reason*,—
> And reasoners, whether clad in pink
> Or red or blue, are on the brink
> (Nine chances out of ten) of treason.

Moore produced altogether a vast number of occasional satirical poems, ranging from easy ridicule to savage denunciation.
They evoked laughter, but some of them also drew blood. Even
George Saintsbury, who called Moore's lighter poems "great
fun, . . . [marked by] acute observation, put into notable form
by an accomplished man of letters," was moved to call some of the
more rancorous ones "turgid rant." [3]

Technically, they show no great innovation; nearly all are in the
familiar iambic tetrameter or pentameter, in couplets or an a-b-a-
b rhyme-pattern. They have, however, style and finish; and the
rhymes, though occasionally outrageous, for the most part are
clever. Hazlitt, who was no friend of their viewpoint, yet conceded their adroitness and "delicate insinuation."

Some of Moore's satirical poems are a mere voicing of amiable prejudice—such as his antifeminist dislike of bluestockings in "A Blue Love Song," in which the "scribbling wife" is told:

> Just think, my own Malthusian dear,
> How much more decent 'tis to hear
> "How is your book?" than "How's your baby?"

Others, like "Tory Pledges," have sharp applicability even today:

> I pledge myself thro' thick and thin
> To labor still with zeal devout
> To get the Outs, poor devils, in,
> And turn the Ins, the wretches, out.

But in a few of the poems Moore rises to the heights of really wounding satire fired by honest anger. When Sir Robert Peel called the Public Debt a "Family Account," Moore proffered, to be sung to a popular tune, a new "pastoral ballad" called "All in the Family Way":

> My labourers used to eat mutton,
> As any great man of the state does;
> And now the poor devils are put on
> Small rations of tea and potatoes.
> But cheer up, John, Sawney, and Paddy,[4]
> The King is your father, they say;
> So ev'n if you starve for your Daddy,
> 'T is all in the family way.

Again, in 1827 the Catholic Emancipation Bill was defeated once more. Immediately five million rounds of cartridges were rushed to all the garrisons in Ireland. Moore responded with "A Pastoral Ballad, by John Bull":

> She [Ireland] askt me for Freedom and Right,
> But ill she her wants understood;—
> Ball cartridges, morning and night,
> Is a dose that will do her more good.

One of the bitterest, and one of the best, of Moore's truly satiric poems is the long "Epistle of Condolence from a Slave-Lord to a

Cotton-Lord." England abolished slavery in its overseas colonies in 1807, but it was 1811 before the slave trade was finally suppressed. The first feeble effort to regulate child labor in textile factories (not in mines or fields) was a law, a mutilated form of a bill introduced by the great reformer, Robert Owen, in 1819. Even this met with loud outcry from the mill-owners. Moore's slave-lord expresses his sympathy:

> Alas! my dear friend, what a state of affairs!
> How unjustly we both are despoiled of our rights!
> Not a pound of black flesh shall I leave to my heirs,
> Nor must *you* any more work to death little whites. . . .
>   Farewell to the zest
> Which slavery now lends to each tea-cup we sip,
> Which makes still the cruellest coffee the best,
> And the sugar the sweetest which smacks of the whip.
> Farewell too the factories' white pickaninnies—
> Small living machines . . . flogged to their tasks.

Like too many of Moore's poems, this loses its vigor toward the end and peters out in near inanity; he would have benefited by the stern editor he never had. But it is evidence that it was not the wrongs of Ireland alone that could awaken his indignation, and that he was capable of verse that slashed deep and left a scar.

V   *The Fudges*

Howard Mumford Jones calls *The Fudge Family in Paris* "the most readable of Moore's satires." [5] It was certainly the most ambitious. In the guise of a series of letters from members of the family to correspondents in England, while (soon after Waterloo) they are enjoying a holiday in Paris, so long forbidden by the Napoleonic Wars to English tourists, it makes fun of both English and Continental politics and economics. Phil Fudge, the father, who seems to be a widower, has been a Tory informer in Ireland, and although now retired is still acting discreetly for Lord Castlereagh. His son Bob is what would then have been called a "noodle"—a dandy whose only interests are in food and clothing —*not* in girls, thanks to Moore's streak of Irish Puritanism where sex was concerned. The daughter, Biddy, is a light-headed scatterbrain and a naïve snob; but despite himself Moore could not keep from giving her a bit of charm, and her letters are by far the best. There is also a tutor, Phelim Connor, a solemn and hortatory young man whose philosophical disquisitions are altogether unreadable; he is a poor relation of the Fudges, and, Biddy confides to her friend Dolly, *"entre nous,* too, a Papist—how liberal of Pa!" What story line there is is Biddy's—her sad awakening when the admirer she had taken for an exiled king or at the very least an army officer turns out to be a shop-clerk.

A good part of *The Fudge Family in Paris* (omitting Phelim's long, drawn-out dissertations, and discounting Phil Fudge's epistles, in the familiar vein of Moore's topical satire) is absolutely first-rate light verse, witty, colloquial, full of verve and gaiety and too good-natured to sting very hard. It displays a masterly command of rhymes, including some dazzling French-English ones. This kind of amiable raillery is, together with his flair for singable lyrics, Moore's real forte. Even the pedantic footnotes, telling his readers things they must already have known, cannot spoil it.

This, like other poems of its sort, Moore brought out as by "Thomas Brown the Younger," but in a facetious preface he reveals openly that "Brown" is Thomas Moore—by way of a Greek pun on his name.[6]

Even boring, rhetorical Phelim Connor occasionally gets off a good line, such as "Hating Napoleon much, but Freedom more." And Phil Fudge, heavy as he is, remarks that

> Europe at the moment
> Enjoys a peace which like the Lord's
> Passeth all human understanding.

But it is Biddy who is given the best role. Here she is, explaining to Dolly that Lord Castlereagh has suggested that Papa write a book:

> A good orthodox book is much wanting just now
> To expound to the world the new—thingummie—science,
> Found out by the—what's-its-name—Holy Alliance;
> And prove to mankind that their rights are but folly,
> Their freedom a joke (which it is, you know, Dolly).

In these poems the iambics march and the anapests skip instead of swooning. Technically, Moore's humorous and satirical verse is often tighter and better controlled than his serious poetry. There are rhymes worthy of Ogden Nash—"dagger a . . . Niagara," "ecstasy . . . neck to see."

Altogether, *The Fudge Family in Paris* was a resounding success and went into edition after edition. The Tory journalists, naturally, did not join in the praise. *The Literary Gazette* said sourly that the poem combined "a flowing versification and a seasoning of witticisms [with] the defamation of statesmen, the insult of monarchs, and the calumny of country." (It did not note that the country "calumniated" was not Moore's own!) An anonymous critic delivered himself of "The Fudges Fudged," to which he wisely did not sign his name:

> A Ballad-singer who had long
> Strummed many a vile lascivious song . . .
> Worn out and impotent become,
> Beats, as he can, sedition's drum.

So well received by most readers, however, was *The Fudge Family in Paris* that seventeen years later Moore followed it with *The Fudge Family in England*. It was a sad come-down. The sprightly gaiety is all gone; the satire is heavy-handed. Phil Fudge is dead; Bob is a self-indulgent old bachelor; Biddy is now a rich old maid hunting for a husband—preferably a young High Church clergyman, for "Time had reduced her to wrinkles and prayers,/And the Flirt found a decent retreat in the Saint." The "saint," however, still has plenty of worldly interests.

She has living with her a beautiful young niece, Fanny, who is a dedicated poetess—her poems sound like bad parodies of Moore himself in his most maudlin vein, and doubtless were deliberately intended to be so, for Moore could sometimes be an acute critic of his own work. Biddy sets her cap for young Patrick Mahan, an Irish gentleman, and deludes herself into thinking he is in love with her instead of (as is of course the case) with Fanny.

Brother Bob appears occasionally, until he has a stroke at news of Catholic Emancipation:

> And whereas, till the Catholic bill,
> I never wanted draught or pill,
> The settling of that curséd question
> Has quite *un*settled my digestion.

There is also the Reverend Mortimer (né Murtagh) O'Mulligan, a renegade Irishman who is now a Protestant preacher. Moore is still incensed by the Church of Ireland and its tithes:

> . . . Rude radicals hector
> At paying some thousands a year to a Rector
> In places where Protestants *never yet were,*
> Who knows but young Protestants *may* be born there? . . .
> And while fools are computing what Parsons would cost,
> Precious souls are meanwhile to the Establishment lost.

Larry O'Branigan, who becomes O'Mulligan's servant, writes to his wife Judy in Irish brogue—the only time Moore attempted this and not too successfully; he himself never spoke with a brogue.

The new Biddy is absurd without being funny, though she does serve as voice for one or two sly digs—"Not *this* world's wedlock —gross, gallant,/But pure—as when Amram married his aunt." Fanny is mostly silly, O'Mulligan is dull except for an occasional sally—

> Ah happy time! when wolves and priests
> Alike were hunted as wild beasts;
> And five pounds was the price, *per* head,
> For bagging *either,* live or dead.

(This is historically true.) Bob, Mahan, and Larry are tough going. By 1835 Moore was very tired, very sad, and lost in the mazes of Irish history. He finished the Fudges off perfunctorily: Mahan elopes with Fanny—first making her promise never to write poetry again—and goes back to Ireland, with Larry as his servant; a great-uncle never before mentioned leaves Fanny his fortune; and Biddy swallows her disappointment and marries

O'Mulligan, who thereupon changes his name to the Reverend Mortimer O'Fudge.

Moore as a satirical poet was about finished. Moreover, by this time he thought of himself chiefly as a prose-writer, although his world had not yet forgotten him as a poet. Before we leave this earlier phase of his literary career, let us discuss those of his poems which have not yet been considered.

CHAPTER 5

Other Poems

I. *Anacreon*

BESIDES his lyrics for songs and the narrative and satiric poems, Moore wrote any number of other short poems—odes, ballads, glees, a miscellany of juvenile versification, and translations or versions of poems in other languages. Chief and earliest of these last was the series of so-called *Odes of Anacreon* —"so-called" because although Anacreon was a genuine Greek poet of the fifth century B.C., the reputed fragments of his work that have come down to us, and which Moore with all his contemporaries took at face value, are probably imitations written from two to nine hundred years after his death. Some of them may actually be his, but all quotations from him imbedded in other authentic Greek works are in Ionic Greek (Anacreon was from Teos in Asia Minor) whereas the fragments on which Moore relied are not; they are in Attic Greek.

All of the presumed Anacreontic imitations, and supposedly the original odes themselves, are a sort of gloss on the theme of "wine, woman, and song." Anacreon was a Greek Omar Khayyám without the Persian astronomer-poet's disenchanted philosophy. What we possess, ostensibly, of his writing presents him as a man in a mellow old age, but still youthful in his feelings. It is amazing how well Thomas Moore, who began the translation when he was still a college student and who was only twenty-one when the *Odes* were published, takes on the *persona* of this ancient rake.

Moore's are not strict translations; indeed, all his verse translations, notably those from the Roman elegiac poets, must be distinguished as "after," not "from," their authors. Nevertheless, a great deal of scholarship went into his Anacreon versions, as evidenced by the copious and learned footnotes. The *Odes* are preceded by "remarks" which embody all then known about the poet, and by an original ode in Greek followed by "corrections" to it "by an eminent Greek scholar." (The eminent scholar is unnamed, and may well have been Moore himself on later reflection.)

Metrically, the *Odes* are not exactly in the Anacreontic form set down by rule by John Phillips in the seventeenth century. Phillips ordained "seven syllables, but in no required meter." Moore's are mostly in iambic tetrameter, which of course has eight syllables. Moreover, Moore's poems are in rhymed couplets, whereas classical Greek (and Latin) poetry knew no rhyme.

But the spirit of the Anacreontic remains or attributions has been caught admirably. L. A. G. Strong was quite right when he called the verses "skillful, fluent, and superficial, with a certain freshness and high spirits." [1] This well describes also the originals themselves from which Moore worked.

As a matter of fact, most of Moore's Anacreontic odes are charming. They are frivolous, to be sure, and occasionally sickeningly saccharine; but nearly all of them, whether they are true to the real Anacreon or not, are delightful reading, which not even the pedantic footnotes can spoil.

It is difficult, in our age of frank speaking, to understand why such harmless gaiety received so much critical censure, or why Moore himself had to deprecate "the careless facility with which Anacreon appears to have trifled." Most of the odes are in the first person, with Anacreon representing himself as a lusty, wine-bibbing old man, who can scarcely "Count me all the flames I prove,/All the gentle nymphs I love." Yet about all he does with the nymphs is to dance with them, walk with them, sit beside them, and perhaps imprint a daring kiss upon a rosy cheek; and his doting descriptions of their beauty seldom go anatomically below their white necks. Sir Edmund Gosse, that epitome of Victorianism, might be expected to have called them erotic, as he did; but the *Odes* appeared thirty-seven years before Victoria ascended the throne—and the Regency is always thought of as an outspoken era. Apparently its candor was coupled with hypocrisy, especially where wives and daughters were concerned!

True, in Moore's verse "a charm may peep, a hue may beam," but only to "leave the rest to Fancy's dream." There is absolutely no explicit sexuality. The nearest Moore comes to it is:

> Oh! may the sun, benignant, shed
> His blandest influence o'er thy bed;
> And foster there an infant tree
> To bloom like her, to tower like thee—

That is a commonplace of all epithalamiums, both classic and Elizabethan. The only truly amorous ode is one which depicts the lover as horse-breaker to the "maid of Thrace" who "like some wanton filly sporting" tries to evade his courtship, to be warned: "Soon shalt thou feel the rein's control/And tremble at the wished-for goal." And it may be doubted, two hundred years before Freud, if Moore himself comprehended the implications of this poem.

One begins to wonder if the real animus of the violent critics was not, rather than Anacreon's weakness for wine and girls, his firm repugnance to war, and his preference for nonmartial songs: "Bacchus shall bid my winter bloom,/And Venus dance me to the tomb." The year 1800 was not a time in which to discount the martial spirit.

II *The "Thomas Little" Poems*

The same accusation—and lack—of explicit eroticism applies both to *The Poetical Works of Thomas Little,* published in 1801, and the *Epistles, Odes, and Other Poems,* five years later.

"Thomas Little" was rather an elaborate hoax which fooled nobody. In a disingenuous preface he is alleged to have died "in his one-and-twentieth year," leaving both these poetic remains and "a novel in rather imperfect state" which Moore as editor promises to revise for publication but of which nothing more was ever heard.

These early poems are full of youthful cynicism about women; they celebrate on-again-off-again passions for Julia, Rosa, Fanny, and other pseudonymous and perhaps imaginary girls; but they are far more literary than they are erotic. The ladies weep and smile and blush and languish, but for all of anything Moore says about them, they remain virgins. These are flirtations rather than serious love-affairs. "To love you was pleasant enough,/And oh! 't is delicious to hate you!"—or again, from *Songs from* [a long way from] *the Greek Anthology:* "I would instantly join my dead love in the tomb—/Unless I could meet with a new one."

It sheds light on the unwholesome hypocrisy of the era that mothers forbade their daughters to read such harmless lines as these, lest they become debauched; and that Francis Jeffrey (before he became Moore's friend and admirer) could thunder that Thomas Moore was "the most licentious of modern versifiers, . . . and the most poetical of those who in our times have devoted their talents to the propagation of immorality," and call him "wantonly voluptuous" and his poems "effeminate" and "fitted for a bagnio." [2]

It is truly a puzzle why these innocuous verses should have aroused such a passion of execration, why they should have been attacked as "the unhallowed fruit of cheap and vulgar prostitution," "a chorus of habitual debauchery," and Moore himself as "a literary pimp," "a pander of posterity" (whatever that means), whose evil aim it is to "impose corruption on his readers."

How far Moore is from any actual eroticism may be seen by comparison of his versions of the Roman elegiac poets, Propertius, Tibullus, and Catullus, with the originals. They are sadly watered down, and where the Latin poet is explicitly obscene, Moore evades and paraphrases. When Byron, in *English Bards and Scotch Reviewers*, hailed Moore as "the young Catullus of his day,/As sweet, but as immoral in his lay," he had forgotten his Catullus. Moore is nowhere as piercingly, lyrically sweet as is the Roman poet—and nowhere nearly so "immoral."

If the diatribes directed against these early poems are puzzling, so also is their overwhelming popularity and the instant fame they brought to the young poet. They are for the most part mere 'prentice work, born of the library, not of the heart, imitative as beginners' poems usually are, technically adroit but otherwise undistinguished.

The singer to come appears in a few fledgling notes. There are foreshadowings of the lilt (and of the sentimentality) of the *Irish Melodies* in some of the lines in these early volumes—"Light sounds the harp when the combat is over"; "When the sad word 'Adieu' from my lip is nigh falling"; "Well, peace to thy heart, though another's it be,/And health to that cheek, though it bloom not for me." [3]

The anapests have made their debut which were to become the hallmark of the *Irish Melodies*. But if his first two or three volumes of poetry had been all Thomas Moore was ever to publish, he would long ago have been completely forgotten.

III *Later Poems*

As for the rest of Moore's miscellanous poetry, it calls for only brief mention. He wrote too much, and too much of what he wrote was mere pedestrian versification. *Alciphron* has been called the most unreadable of Moore's poems, but *Rhymes for the Road,* a dull travelogue in rocking-horse rhythm, runs it a close second. None of the *Ballads and Songs* is up to the *Irish Melodies* or even to the *National Airs.* The *Legendary Ballads,* some of them based on such well-worn legends as those of Cupid and Psyche and Hero and Leander, some on themes less known, or perhaps original with Moore, are agreeable but not memorable; the best of them, because of metric interest and a certain haunting quality, are "The Voice" and "The Stranger." *The Summer Fête* is heavy going.

The most that can be said of most of these miscellaneous lyrical and seminarrative poems is that they are good occasional verse, competent and doubtlessly appealing to its sentimental public. As with the juvenile volumes, if they had been all that Moore wrote, he would never have been heard of after his death.

The best of the later poems is *Evenings in Greece,* inspired by the Greek Revolution. Apparently it was intended for some kind of private performance, for Moore points out that the poetical narrative is meant to be recited, "so as to enable a greater number of persons to join"; it is interspersed with songs for those "willing or competent to take part as singers."

The scene is the Island of Zea (Cos), and the time is roughly contemporary. The men are at war, on leave, or just returned from war; and many of the songs are martial ones. Others are love songs, or songs of loss and sorrow sung by the girls the soldiers have left behind, with touches of nature rare in Moore:

> Here, while the moonlight dim
> Falls on that mossy brim,
> Sing we our Fountain Hymn,
> Maidens of Zea!

The poem contains one of Moore's few poetic allusions to Byron:

> Sad Missilonghi,[4] sorrowing yet
> O'er him, the noblest Star of Fame
> That e'er in life's young glory set!

Evenings in Greece, like the *Legendary Ballads,* is marred by pedantry and rhetoric. Both belong to a time when Moore was ceasing to find in poetry his main mode of literary expression.

One other of his miscellaneous poems calls for comment, not because it is good poetry, for it is not, but because it was one of the few he wrote which alluded simply and sincerely to his own day-to-day life. It also contains one of his rare tributes to his faithful wife.[5] It is "My Birth-Day."

> Those friendships, in my boyhood twined,
> And kept till now unchangeingly;
> And that dear home, that saving ark,
> Where Love's true light at last I've found,
> Cheering within, when all grows dark
> And comfortless and stormy round!

Gradually the poet was being transformed into the prose-writer, the ebullition of youth into the sobriety of middle age. To the world he might still be "Melody Moore," but to himself he was the dutiful, professional biographer.

CHAPTER 6

The Biographies

I *Moore as Biographer*

MOORE was by nature a poet—or even more, a minstrel; but he was by profession an author who earned his living and supported his family mainly by his writing. He had already published a good deal of prose before he undertook his first biography, but it had been mostly in the field of journalism or of polemics in the Irish cause. His only major prose work before his life of Sheridan was the *Memoirs of Captain Rock,* which belongs in the latter category.

He was, in fact, not too well fitted to become a biographer. He was a man of letters, something of a pedant, but not in the true sense a scholar. He was accustomed to research in libraries, but not to the consultation of first-hand sources; conscientiously he sought the interviews with relatives and associates which a biography of a recently deceased person involves, but his findings were too often merely inserted, unevaluated and undigested, into his narrative.

Moreover, his was not a good time for biography as we understand it today. It was a period when, soon after the death of a celebrated man, there issued from the press a huge multivolumed "Life and Letters," which laboriously took its subject chronologically from his ancestry to his funeral. It consisted for the most part of quotations from or reprintings of his speeches and correspondence, and of his diary if he kept one. It made little attempt to present him in his private aspect, or to view him objectively. It was usually an official eulogy, mealy-mouthed; evasive of any shadows on his life or character; and entirely non-critical; and the result was a dull and stodgy work. All these characteristics, which in our day critics would consider gross faults, were the necessary requirements of any authorized biography in the early part of the nineteenth century. All of them appear, in greater or less degree, in Moore's three biographies—of Richard Brinsley Sheridan, of Lord Byron, and of Lord Edward Fitzgerald.

One of Moore's subjects was a close friend and an outstanding figure in the literature of his era and indeed of all time. Another was a man who had won his youthful romantic admiration but whom he had never known and had seen once only, when as a boy he passed him on a Dublin street. The other was a man he had known fairly well, had admired and pitied, but on several counts had not much approved of. In all Moore's biographies he was accused by some critics of triviality and superficiality, and by others of bias. The criticisms are not entirely fair: Moore was never profound, but he tried hard, so far as the literary customs of his day permitted, to present his subjects seriously and sincerely; and the accusations of bias were based on political disagreement.

To a certain extent, however, these strictures do obtain, particularly in his first biography, that of Sheridan. The book was written, not from an overwhelming impulse to pay tribute to the dramatist and statesman, but because a publisher offered him the assignment and paid him to carry it out. With the life of Fitzgerald, there *was* personal impetus: it was the culmination and the conclusion of his close connection with the Irish question. And in the case of his life of Byron, he was taken for granted as the proper choice—though, as we shall see, there were painful complications.

Half a hack-writer Moore may have been, and not altogether qualified as a biographer even by the standards of his own day: but no one who reads his Journal can fail to be impressed by the conscientiousness and diligence with which he sought out every acquaintance of his subject, besieged them for information, noted for future use every anecdote or recollection, however unimportant. Often his task became as much detection as it was research. Here, for example, is a typical entry: "Much talk . . . got little more. Am very glad, however, I came, as I should have reproached myself for not having done so, and others would have reproached me also." Often he made long journeys, merely to find someone who might just possibly have something new to tell him.

In the biography of Sheridan, he had two handicaps. The first, which slowed up perceptibly the writing of the book, was his exile in France, which made it impossible for him to see and talk to persons without whom he could not consider his preparation for the work properly accomplished; for the second, he had to contend with his distaste for his subject's private life. In the life of Byron, he met with the opposition of Byron's widow, his half-sister, and his jealous friends. In the Fitzgerald book, he was faced with the difficulty that most of the people who had immediate knowledge of Fitzgerald were either dead or in far parts of the world.

Yet he did triumph over all these obstacles—most especially in the life of Byron—and if these massive two-volume works are not to our current taste, they were very much to the taste of his contemporaries.

II *Sheridan*

Moore and Sheridan were familiar acquaintances but never intimate friends. Sheridan was twenty-eight years his senior, for one thing, and Moore was out of sympathy with his subject for several reasons. He disapproved highly of Sheridan's continuing closeness to the Regent, which he viewed as wrong-headed and sycophantic —though he was outraged by the Regent's ingratitude and neglect of Sheridan in the latter's impecunious last days.

The rumors that spread of the playwright's dire need, which aroused Moore's generous indignation, were exaggerated, although it is true enough that Sheridan was very hard up and that his rich friends did little to help him. It is also true that the Regent contemptuously awarded his former boon companion a mere "pitance" in the way of a pension—when it was too late, and was refused. Immediately after these stories reached his ears, Moore wrote his irate "Lines on the Death of Sheridan," excoriating the royal ingrate and all the rest of Sheridan's fair-weather friends:

> How proud they can press to the funeral array
> Of one whom they shunned in his sickness and sorrow:
> How bailiffs may seize his last blanket to-day,
> Whose pall shall be held up by nobles to-morrow!

But, besides his dislike of Sheridan's extravagance and philandering, Moore could not forget that Sheridan *had* failed to repudiate the Regent when the future George IV turned his coat on

the Irish questions. Still, Sheridan had been one of the few Members of Parliament who had always opposed the Union between England and Ireland. He could not, moreover, be denied credit for the great speeches which led to the impeachment of Warren Hastings.[1] Rather grudgingly, Moore conceded that Sheridan had entered politics "when habits of business or a knowledge of details was less looked for in public men, . . . when the House of Commons was . . . a more open play-ground for eloquence and wit." [2]

To his contemporaries, Sheridan was primarily the orator and parliamentarian. To us, he is remembered as the author of *The Rivals, The School for Scandal,* and perhaps *The Critic,* and to a lesser degree as the part-owner and director of Drury Lane Theater. This dichotomy in his life resulted, in Moore's painstaking effort to give a full account of his subject's public career, in a rather broken-backed book—the first, or theatrical, portion lively and entertaining, the later, or political, part heavy and overdetailed, stuffed with the minutiae of causes and personages now equally dead. Sheridan was a brilliant orator, but nothing is so dull as forgotten political issues.

Where Moore can wholeheartedly admire and approve, he does so with good will. He calls *The School for Scandal* "the best comedy in the language," he applauds its "triumph of taste and skill," notes its combination of ease and polish, "at the same time, idiomatic and elegant," its "perpetual play of wit combined with almost faultless finish." He does not abdicate as a critic; he recognizes that there is "little interest in the plot, no very profound or ingenious development of character"—indeed, that none of the characters "has any legitimate claims upon either our affection or our esteem." Yet, he adds, "how perfect must be the work in which no greater fault can be found." [3]

He does not think so highly of *The Rivals,* which he considers "by no means so pointed or sparkling." [4] He differentiates between Sheridan's "witty and serious styles—the occasional effort of the one and the too frequent false finery of the other." [5] But in the end he concludes that Sheridan's wit, "like the laurel of Caesar, was leafy enough to hide any bareness." [6]

Yet, much as he admired Sheridan as an author, Moore could not hide his basic distaste for the man. Priggishly he speaks of

Sheridan's "social qualities, [which] were, unluckily for himself, but too attractive."[7] He could sympathize with Sheridan's financial difficulties—he too was no businessman, he too knew the burden of debt. Yet Moore was not extravagant, he did not live beyond his means; and Sheridan was and did. In Moore's frequent forays into the great and gay world of London from his quiet cottage in the country, he knew the pleasures of Society; but he did not spend his whole time in that Vanity Fair or let it seduce him from responsibility, as Sheridan did.

And especially, as the devoted husband who never looked elsewhere, he disapproved of Sheridan's reputed roving eye. This Irish poet who was accused of "lasciviousness" and "voluptuousness" actually had a broad streak of puritanism in his nature. He realized and acknowledged Sheridan's ardent love for his first wife (with whom he had eloped and for whom he had fought two duels), but he could not countenance the dramatist's submersion into the hard-drinking, free-loving world of the Regent and his court. Try as he might, he could not keep a note of censure from his tones: "Such a career as this—so shaped towards wrong, so inevitably devious—it would be impossible—it is impossible to regard otherwise than with the most charitable allowance."[8]

This being so, Moore realized that he could not altogether please Sheridan's friends. Frankly, he said as much: "'I seek truth,' said an ancient,[9] 'by which nobody ever yet was injured'—except, sometimes, (he might have added,) those who venture to *tell* it. . . . By an impartial view of the faults, as well as merits, of all parties, I had but little chance of gaining the good will of any. The latter was, however, the plan that I adopted."[10]

This declaration strikes the modern reader as amusing, in view of the actual reticence of Moore's biography. He has been accused of not making full use of the papers to which Sheridan's family gave him access; but if this is so, it was not from lack of scholarliness but from unwillingness to go too far into details of a career which he disapprobated. Moore, always eager not to offend, in any event preferred silence to unfavorable comment. We are accustomed to "debunking," to open discussion of the most private affairs of a dead and helpless man. Moore's time was not. *Nobody* then wrote what we would call a full and candid biography.

Moore's avowed ideal was the candid "new biography," modeled on Boswell's *Life of Johnson*. However, we know a great deal about Samuel Johnson now that Boswell would never have dreamed of putting into print. To some readers today, a modicum of that "decent reticence" then taken for granted does not seem to be altogether mistaken.

But the consequence of this attitude is that in Moore's biography of Sheridan we have a conscientious, documented (too well-documented) account, as sympathetic as he could make it—but one that is without depth, and that lacks, to modern eyes, the very fire and sparkle which made its subject so eminent. Like all nineteenth-century biographies it is strictly chronological in pattern: birth, education, career, death; with solid chunks of unedited letters inserted whole. That is the way its first readers expected a biography to be, and they never envisioned any other possibility.

The result is that the *Memoirs of Sheridan* (to shorten its title) exists, a century and a half after its publication, as a source-book for later biographers and as little more. Only John Drinkwater has praised it in modern times. And even in Moore's own time it was considered quite inferior to his life of Byron.

One contributing factor is that it was nine years in the writing (Sheridan died in 1816), and the most of it was written while its author was undergoing the strain, harassment, and apprehension arising from the defalcation of his deputy in Bermuda. One may ask, then, why he wrote the book at all.

One reason, of course, was obvious: he needed the money. Originally intended for publication by Murray, Longmans took it over for £1000 when Moore had to delay finishing it until he could return to England from France and carry on the necessary interviews. The other reason lies deeper, in a mixture of innocent vanity and justified ambition. It became before the end an onerous task, and he confided to his diary that one of his friends thought "I shall have a good escape of it if my Life of Sheridan is given up." Nevertheless he labored on. And why? Because, he told his journal—but then he always expected his journal to be published ultimately, so he never wrote anything in it that he wanted never to appear in print—people had always said that he "could write pretty songs, and launch a smart epigram, but that there is nothing solid in him." Now Jeffrey, whose opinion he respected, was encouraging him to undertake a "solid" work. Jeffrey thought it "a work of great importance to my fame." Jeffrey read the manuscript and reported that it gave "convincing proof that you can reason solidly and manfully. . . . I look upon the part of your book that relates to Sheridan himself as comparatively worthless: it is for the historical and political views that I value it." [11] In other words, the "valuable" part of the book is the very part that now seems superfluous and extraneous! It is a strange commentary on a work that ostensibly is entirely devoted to "Sheridan himself." But to Moore, coming from Jeffrey, it was an acclamation.

III *Byron*

Very different indeed was his attitude toward the biography of Byron; and very different was the book that resulted. With the present neglect of Thomas Moore, it is easy to wonder why he should have been the obvious choice as Byron's official biographer. It came as no surprise to his contemporaries. He was, after Byron, the best known poet of his day—far better known to the general public than, say, Wordsworth or Coleridge, or than Keats and Shelley had been before their deaths shortly before. He was, besides, known as Byron's intimate friend; if there was any disparity between their affection for each other, it was Byron who was the loving friend and Moore who was the loved.

Furthermore, he was the man to whom Byron had given his manuscript memoirs—a trust which had been torn from him. Against his vain protests, he had seen the manuscript destroyed. The contretemps, besides his personal offense and regret, had put him heavily in debt to John Murray, a debt that could be discharged only by writing a book that could earn him that much money.

He felt that his sacrifice entitled him to the opportunity. He had tried hard to redeem the memoirs before and immediately after Byron's death. He could not borrow the sum from any of his wealthy noble friends; both Lord Lansdowne and Lord Holland, for example, objected to publication of the memoirs—especially Holland, whose wife had been rumored to be one of Byron's mistresses. Moore had protested the burning to the last, as "contradictory to Lord Byron's wishes and unjust to me," but he had been overruled; and he felt it better to acquiesce than to allow the slightest shadow of suspicion on his own motives. As Doris Langley Moore has said, he "had parted with a sum insanely beyond his means to pay for a measure which he had angrily opposed, and which had turned out after all to involve property not his own." [12]

He had endured Hobhouse's sneer that "Lord Byron made a present of himself to Mr. Moore, and Mr. Moore sold his Lordship to the booksellers," though Hobhouse very well knew that in 1821 Byron had stated that Moore's disposal of the memoirs to Murray had his entire approval.[13] Hobhouse had alleged that Byron had thought better of his generosity, and wanted to recall the manuscript but refrained because he did not wish to hurt Moore's feelings. Moore wrote Hobhouse and asked him for any proof whatever of that allegation—and received no reply. (Hobhouse, Doris Langley Moore suggests, resented Moore's "advertising to the world an intimacy with Byron which might be thought to eclipse his own.")[14] Moore had legitimate cause to feel it his *right* to be chosen as Byron's biographer, however much Lady Byron, Augusta Leigh, Hobhouse, or anyone else might object.

And underneath everything else, there may well have lurked an understandable subconscious jealousy of Byron's immense fame. He considered himself Byron's equal as a poet—and Byron would have agreed. After all, if Moore had died first, Byron might very well have been asked to write *his* biography.

In the end, the book he wrote justified him. True, just as in the biography of Sheridan, there was much in Byron's life that Moore suppressed. (His book itself would have been suppressed if he had not done so, as Howard Mumford Jones points out.[15] In England, proof of the truth of defamatory assertions is no defense in a suit for criminal libel. And can one imagine Lady Caroline Lamb, for example, refraining from suing if Moore had mentioned even a tenth of the remarks that Byron had given vent to concerning her and their liaison?)

This kind of voluntary censorship is an offense to present literary ethics, but decidedly was not so in the early nineteenth century. Moore did inexcusably destroy all Byron's letters after he had used them (even those lent him by others), but this also must have seemed justified in his eyes. He not only omitted, he also garbled (often at Murray's "suggestion," which was equivalent to an order), so that by modern standards the book is not altogether a reliable guide. Nevertheless, Richard Garnett says justly that it is a work "reticent but not insincere, . . . exactly the biography which the age and the circumstances required." [16]

Even if these cogent reasons had not obtained, Moore's own canons would have made him shrink from revelation of the more unsavory episodes of Byron's career. Doris Langley Moore remarks that Moore was firmly of the opinion that *Don Juan* was "unpublishable," and had told Byron so! [17] It is now considered by accepted critics to be Byron's greatest poem.

As might have been expected, the biography, when it appeared, aroused Lady Byron's wrath; no biography would have suited her save one she had written herself. She wrote an indignant letter, mostly concerned with defending her parents and members of their household from Byron's opinion of them, and Moore included it as an appendix in a later edition. Augusta Leigh was also offended; as was her wont, she said nothing publicly, but confided in private letters how angry she was. (Moore, poor man, met her at a party and wrote in his journal that she seemed to like him: Augusta was a mistress of social dissembling.) But even Hobhouse had to acknowledge that Moore's portrayal of Byron's personality was fair. And Macaulay, who as a Tory was always quick to condemn anything written by Moore or his circle, was handsome enough in his praise of the writing itself: "Considered merely as a composition, it deserves to be classed among the best specimens of English prose which our age has produced. The style is agreeable, clear, and manly, and when it rises into eloquence, rises without effort or ostentation." [18] The general critical consensus was overwhelmingly favorable.

It remains so among present-day commentators. L. A. G. Strong believes that "in this book Moore's prose attained a dignity and a weight it had not hitherto reached." [19] And Howard Mumford Jones goes so far as to call the biography of Byron "one of the four or five great literary biographies in the English language." [20] He thinks it "the one book by which Moore lives today." [21]

To a certain extent, this latter judgment is true: in so far as anyone reads any whole book of Moore's today, it is likely to be this one. But if we judge it by the standards of, say, Boswell's *Life of Johnson,* it must be relegated to a lesser rank. It has great virtues: it is clear, easy in style, readable on every page, studiously objective instead of merely adulatory of a friend, as so many "Lives and Letters" in that day were.

No one else who could write as well as Moore was as close to Byron. As Strong says, "The scores are even. Moore failed to prevent one wrong to Byron's memory, but he did a great deal to preserve and safeguard what remained. [Imagine, for example, how different a Life might have been, written by Leigh Hunt!] On the other side, were it not for Byron, Moore would be less than he is. Among his chief claims to remembrance is his association [with Byron]." [22]

The general reader, however, who approaches this two-volume work not as a student, but simply for enjoyment, may well be intimidated by Moore's apparatus—by the fact that in the sense to which we have grown accustomed this is not a biography at all. The exact title is *The Letters and Journals of Lord Byron: with Some Notices of His Life*—and that is exactly what it is. The letters and the extracts from the journals are put in their proper chronological place; they have been edited (sometimes too much so); but the general effect is—as Moore intended—to let Byron speak for himself. Since Byron was one of the great letter-writers of all time, and was completely uninhibited in his journals, this is all good reading; but it is not a biography in our modern meaning of the word. "It is magnificent, but it is not war." A modern biographer would use, allude to, and quote from his sources rather than present them *in toto,* as Moore often does. This is *not,* however, a modern biography, and it would be foolish to judge Moore by the standards of our age instead of by those of his own. It is thanks largely to his book on Byron that for the last quarter century of his life Moore was thought of primarily as a biographer (though the memory of "Melody Moore" was never extinguished).

Moore himself was well aware of the formidable difficulties facing him when he undertook this work. In the preface to the first volume, which came out almost a year before the second, he spoke diffidently of his "sincere distrust of my own powers of doing justice to such a task," and in the preface to Volume II he mentioned modestly the success of his desire to write objectively—as evidenced, he said, by the very attacks against the first volume. Those attacks, indeed, were never directed against the style in which the book was written, but were either politically inspired or were of the nature of Lady Byron's self-defensive letter. The animus of this letter was apparent in its sneers about "one who claims to be considered as Lord Byron's confidential and authorised friend," and its allegation that Moore had "promulgated his own impressions, . . . as if he possessed a competent knowledge of the subject." [23] In other words, Lady Byron was angered by the unkind reflections made on her and her family—but quite oblivious to the fact that those reflections had been made, not by Moore, but by Byron himself in quoted letters!

Moore modestly ascribed the success of Volume I to "the interest of the subject and the materials, not to any merit of the editor." He thought of himself throughout as *editing* the work, not as being its author. He acknowledged that he had made "little critical examination" into Byron's poetry—the one thing that would most engage an author today writing about a poet—and indeed, despite "the delight which, in common with all, I derive from his poetry," he believed that "this evading, if it must be so considered, [is] one of my duties as a biographer." [24] This is surely a strange idea to a modern reader. He pleaded besides "my own inaptitude as a critic"—a deprecation which was an instance of either real or false modesty; Moore was an excellent critic, within the limitations of his interests, and must surely have realized it.

His own summing up, at the end of Volume II, was that "I have now done with the subject, nor shall be easily tempted to recur to it. . . . I have here told what I myself know and think concerning my friend, and now leave his character, moral as well as literary, to the judgment of the world." [25]

The world has not judged Byron solely on the evidence of Moore's biography, by any means; but without Moore our first-hand information about Byron would be very much less than it is. As he and his contemporaries understood the writing of biography, he had produced a major work, redounding to the fame of his subject as well as to his own.

IV *Fitzgerald*

Moore's only other biography was *The Life and Death of Lord Edward Fitzgerald*. He had been asked to write the biography of the statesman George Canning, but refused: he was in political disagreement with Canning and would have felt obliged to criticize him harshly; members of Canning's family had been personally kind to him, and characteristically he could not bear to hurt them.

Moore had been Byron's intimate friend; Sheridan he had known well, if not familiarly; but the reason for his book on Fitzgerald, whom he had never met and had even seen only once when he was a child of twelve, lay in his reawakened zeal for the Irish cause. His Whig friends were again in control of the government, and Moore rejoiced. "Instead of having to contend . . . with rulers pledged against her [Ireland's] interests by a system traditionally hostile to all liberal principles, my country now sees in the seats of authority men whose whole lives and opinions are a sufficient security that under their influence better counsels will prevail." [26] He was to be disappointed, but at the time he was very hopeful.

The Whig victory did not activate his book, but it accelerated it. He had long contemplated writing about Fitzgerald, and actually began work on the biography while he was still finishing his life of Byron, making two trips to Ireland at least partly to obtain material for it.

Fitzgerald was one of the most appealing of the leaders of the revolt of the United Irishmen in 1798. Yet it seems strange that Moore did not instead wish to write about his friend Robert Emmet, a much greater man and equally a martyr to the Irish cause. But Emmet, like Edward Hudson, had been a democrat as much as he was a rebel; Fitzgerald was purely a nationalist, and his sole rebellion had been against English rule in Ireland. He had fought with the British in America during the American Revolution. And then Moore did "dearly love a lord." Fitzgerald was young, attractive, domestically virtuous, and he had died bravely for Ireland—also he was the son of the Duke of Leinster and the grandson of the Duke of Richmond. Moore devoted a good deal of his early pages to tracing his Lordship's ancestry.

Yet his life of Fitzgerald is more a political history than it is a genuine biography of one particular man. Most of it is told indirectly, in the form of letters by Fitzgerald, his family, and his friends. Even the affecting story of Fitzgerald's last days, as he lay dying of wounds received in the attack, is told by Moore not as straight description, but through the medium of letters from one member of his family to another. The book is far too full of undigested material, evidence of thorough research but repugnant to all but scholars. Moore knew this, and adopted this method deliberately; he said that the amount of detailed information he was able to present "renders any further comment [of his own] . . . almost wholly superfluous." [27]

There are no chapter divisions in either of the two volumes; the only way we can determine where we are in Fitzgerald's career is by the date at the top of each page. There is little attempt to concentrate on the more salient events of that career, and too much extraneous matter is included which only obfuscates the uninformed reader. Knowledge of both English and Irish history is taken for granted, to a degree that may well have been beyond the public of the time when the book was published, and certainly is beyond that of anyone but a specialist today.

One can scarcely agree with Stephen Gwynn that the *Life and Death of Fitzgerald* is "the best of Moore's prose writing." [28] But one must grant it clarity and directness. And when occasionally Moore does speak in his own voice, the turgid narrative begins to move: allowing for differences between the novelistic style of Moore's day and ours, some few parts of the book, though soundly based on fact, read almost like good realistic fiction. The pity is that Moore did not realize this and take the time to apply the same method to the whole two volumes.

Moore had not gone very far into the book when he began to realize how differently he felt and thought now from the boy who had been heart and soul with the rebels of the "the '98." He began to have qualms about too great identification with them. "Of the right of the oppressed to resist . . . few would venture to express a doubt. . . . To be able to fix, however, . . . the point at which obedience may cease, and resistance to the undue stretches of authority begin, is a difficulty which must for ever leave vague and undirected the application of the principle." [29]

There speaks the man in his forties, the man who has known honor and fame and the friendship of the great. Yet the true Thomas Moore bursts such bonds, and speaks with noble indignation at persecution and injustice: "The government that could drive such a man into such resistance . . . is convicted by this

very result alone, without any further inquiry into its history." [30]
There speaks the "born rebel," who as a boy in college had risked
his future rather than betray his friends.

Few would care to read the biography of Fitzgerald today except those with a specialized interest in Irish history in the late
eighteenth century. Fitzgerald was after all a minor figure, and
this is a minor book. Moore as a biographer, however, is not to be
brushed off with a patronizing word. Even in the Fitzgerald book
there are a few passages, more in the Sheridan one, and many in
the life of Byron, of which no writer of biography need be
ashamed.

Just as in Moore's poems there are lines (seldom complete
poems) which place him almost in the first rank of poetry, so in
these books there are sentences and paragraphs which place him
almost in the first rank of biographers. He could not keep consistently to this standard—but how many writers can? Moore was not
altogether undeserving of the vast acclaim which was his during
his lifetime and for half a century after it. In prose he did relatively little of equal value to the best of his poetry, and his last
prose work was a catastrophe. But no history of English literature
is complete which ignores Thomas Moore the prose writer, as well
as the singer of melodious verse. Two at least of his other books in
prose are worthy of serious consideration.

CHAPTER 7

Other Prose

I *The History of Ireland*

IN GENERAL, Thomas Moore's prose writing falls into two categories: books written because he had something to say and wanted to say it and books written because he earned his living and supported his family by his pen. This statement by no means implies, however, that the former were always superior to the latter. Of the biographies, one may say that Fitzgerald fell under the first classification, Sheridan under the second, and Byron under a mixture of the two. *The Memoirs of Captain Rock, the Travels of an Irish Gentleman in Search of a Religion,* probably *The Epicurean,* and certainly his *Journal* had their origin in his own interests and views (though he always expected and said that his diaries and correspondence should be published and earn money for his dependents after he was dead). Many of his shorter journalistic pieces, certainly his one musical play, *M.P., or the Blue-Stocking,* and above all the *History of Ireland,* would never have existed had they not been commissioned. Despite Moore's love for his native land, he would never of his own volition have undertaken to write a detailed four-volume history of it. It was a chore from the beginning; and in the end it was a killing chore—and a failure.

Originally the Reverend Dyonisius Lardner conceived the idea of what he called *Lardner's Cabinet Cyclopaedia,* which was projected as a series of short histories and other informative books addressed to the semieducated. It was a period when people were just beginning to think of lectures and classes and books for workingmen who were literate but had had only a few years of schooling—not ordinary common laborers, but skilled workmen in the burgeoning Industrial Era.

Sir Walter Scott did the first volume, on the history of Scotland. It was an unpretentious book, simple and well within the scope of the project and the comprehension of the uninformed reader. Then Sir James Mackintosh undertook the history of England. He went all out, and produced a detailed, scholarly, authoritative work that set far too high a standard for the series Lardner had had in mind. So Longmans, who were publishing the series, and Lardner as editor, abandoned the original approach, and decided to transform the *Cabinet Cyclopaedia* into a much more elaborate collection of volumes written by eminent authors. When the question came up of a history of Ireland, the name that immediately suggested itself was that of Thomas Moore.

Moore was utterly unfitted to take on such an assignment. Knowing no Gaelic, he was unable to consult any first-hand documents and was obliged to rely on second-hand translations and accounts. Though he had in the past become accustomed to doing a great deal of research for the *Odes of Anacreon*, for *Lalla Rookh*, for the biographies, and indeed for all his longer or collected works, it was not *historical* research, and he was completely untrained in historical method.

He slaved away without even knowing always where the material he needed was to be found, or if it existed at all. It is no wonder he himself said: "For the first time in my life I feel myself a thorough *hack*." He tried to get out from under the burden, but Longmans had already advertised the work widely—and had already paid him a large advance.

The history was planned to be in four volumes. Volume I came out in 1835, and reached only to the seventh century A.D.! Volume II, in 1837, found Moore still bogged down in the Middle Ages. This meant that the remaining history, up to current times, would have to be scamped and hurried. He managed to finish Volume III by 1840; but it took him six years more to get out the final volume; and when it was done he was so exhausted that he found himself unable to write a preface to it, and had to ask Longmans to get someone else to do the job.

The *Cabinet Cyclopaedia* was disastrous for all the contributors to its historical portions. (The authors of books on the physical sciences, such as Sir William Herschel and Augustus DeMorgan, were more fortunate.) Scott had a stroke soon after, from which he never really recovered; Mackintosh died suddenly; and Moore underwent a serious illness which ended in premature senility.

The History of Ireland did not actually kill him, of course—it was a time of personal tragedy for him, and his illness was not just nervous exhaustion but seems to have been a kind of influenza—but the eleven years of grinding toil contributed their share towards his disastrous end.

After all this drudgery, what he had to show for it was the poorest and dullest of his books. Any conventional history written in the middle of the nineteenth century would seem dull and heavy to modern readers. Moore's was heavy without being authoritative; it could not even serve as a reliable source-book. W. F. P. Stockley calls it "an impossible history," [1] and it is.

It was the first of Moore's books to fall completely flat and to receive very little critical attention. What criticism there was, was censorious and hostile, pointing out its confusion, its unfilled gaps, its overelaboration in some portions and undue skimping in others. Echoing Richard Garnett, who said Moore "failed with a hopeless subject," Ruth L. Johnson called the *History of Ireland* "a dull and dreary work." [2] It must be mentioned in any study of Moore's writing, but otherwise it is deservedly forgotten.

II *Captain Rock*

The Memoirs of Captain Rock is a very different kind of book. It grew out of Moore's deepest convictions and most powerful feelings, fired anew by his first-hand glimpse, on his journey to Ireland with Lansdowne in 1823, of the desperate poverty and degradation to which English rule had reduced the Irish peasants.

"Captain Rock" himself is a folk myth. When the downtrodden Irish revolted and rioted, burned hayricks and sometimes country houses, sometimes attacked their English landlords (or more likely, the latter's Anglo-Irish Protestant stewards), they answered, when apprehended and questioned, that they were "Captain Rock's men." Rock became a sort of combined Robin Hood and Paul Bunyan, and perhaps some of the more simple of his "followers" believed that he was or had been an actual person. The full title of Moore's book is: *The Memoirs of Captain Rock, the Celebrated Irish Chieftain, with some Account of His Ancestors*—and the "ancestors" are the anonymous leaders of earlier revolts all the way back to the time of Henry VIII.

As Howard Mumford Jones says, the book was "almost Swiftian" in its suave sardonicism overlying hot fury at injustice. It created an immediate sensation in both England and Ireland. To some Englishmen in high places it brought home a dreadful situation they had hitherto ignored. Naturally, to the opponents of Catholic Emancipation the book was anathema. One Church of England clergyman called it "a most pestilent and detestable book." Other critics damned it with faint praise; it was, they said, "lively," or "flashy," but its tone did not fit its subject. But in Ireland the poor put together their meager shillings to buy jointly owned copies, and it went into a second edition within a month.

In England too there were not lacking those with the courage to praise it. One was Moore's friend, Sydney Smith, the celebrated wit, "the Smith of Smiths," who, though himself an Anglican priest, said boldly in the *Edinburgh Review* in 1824: "This agreeable [*sic*] and witty book is supposed to have been written by Mr. Thomas Moore, a gentleman . . . full of genius, and a steady friend of all that is honourable and just. . . . The picture he has drawn is at once piteous and frightful. Its effect in exciting our horror and indignation is increased . . . by the tone of levity, and even jocularity, under which he has chosen to veil the deep sarcasm and substantial horrors of his story." [3]

Ironically Moore points out "what good use was made" of the years of English domination of Ireland before the Reformation "in attaching the people to their English governors, and by what a gentle course of alteratives they [the Irish] were prepared for the inoculation of a new religion, which was about to be attempted on them by the same skilful and friendly hands." [4] Then he recites the horrible story of Irishmen dispossessed and deprived of all civil rights, treated not as human beings but as a mere living source of revenue, and of their priests, from Elizabeth I's time onward, hunted like wild beasts, with a bounty on their heads.

At the time of *Captain Rock's* publication Parliament was debating not only Catholic Emancipation but also the formal Union of Ireland and England. The two were interrelated but not inseparable. Moore himself, at least in his persona of Captain Rock, "was assured that a Union will put Emancipation farther off than ever. . . . Promises are put on only to betray. . . . [The Irish] are insulted as well as proscribed, for adherence to their faith, and in every walk of life branded as serfs and outcasts." [5]

Smith concludes his review by remarking that "almost the only persons zealously opposed to the general baseness and fatuity are a few Whigs and Reviewers, or here and there a virtuous poet like Mr. Moore." [6]

So long as indifference to persecution exists, the persecuted will rebel. His father, Captain Rock tells us, taught him as a youth that "we have power on our side that 'will not willingly let us die,' and . . . the family of the Rocks will continue to flourish in all their native glory." "So long the merry reign shall be/Of Captain Rock and his Family."

Moore's object, of course, was not merely to shock his readers, but to reform them. No book could do very much to relieve so vast a tyranny, involving the fortunes of so many powerful men, and intrenched for so many centuries. There was soon thereafter some slight alleviation of the crushing debt-collection system in Ireland (but not of the tithes to the Established Church), but that was little enough. Perhaps a few absentee landlords here and there had their consciences pricked and did what they could— short of cutting their incomes too much—to make their tenants' lives more bearable. Catholic Emancipation was still five years in the future.

The Memoirs of Captain Rock did, however, have two important results, no matter how little it was able to accomplish in the way of wholesale reform. It gave Moore a chance to unburden his heart of its weight of bitterness and frustrated rage. And it proved that, if he were sufficiently aroused, he was quite capable of writing slashing, blood-letting satire, and chilly, precisely aimed irony, in prose as well as or even more than in verse.

III   *Moore as Theologian*

The *Travels of an Irish Gentleman in Search of a Religion* was a completely different kind of work from *Captain Rock*, but equally one written from the depth of emotion. Moore was, as we have seen, a very latitudinarian variety of Christian, and far from a practicing member of the faith in which he was born. Yet in the broadest sense he might be called a religious man. He had a keen interest in questions of religion, and a natural turn for the study of theology.

His pen had fought hard for the cause of Catholic Emancipation, and in a way the *Travels* might be viewed as his method of celebration of final passage of the bill in 1829. He is by no means the "Irish Gentleman" who is the book's protagonist, but it is written in the first person, largely in the form of letters, and often it is apparent that Moore himself is speaking through the semifictional veil.

The book begins, rather oddly, with a Declaration of Independence. Hitherto, while his countrymen were oppressed and persecuted for adherence to their church, as a patriot he had no choice, the narrator says, but to adhere to it also, without examination of his private beliefs. Now "I found myself free, not only from the penalties attached to being a Catholic, but from the point of honour which till then deterred me from being anything else. . . . The relations of my creed with this world had been of too stormy a nature to leave me much thought to bestow on its concernments with the next." [7]

Therefore, the "Irish Gentleman" goes on, he may now, if he so desires, become a Protestant with good conscience. He does not for a moment consider abandoning Christianity for any other creed, or for none: he must as a matter of course be either Catholic or Protestant. (It may be noted that "Catholic" to Moore meant "Roman Catholic"; he discounted or may never have known the fact that both the Eastern Orthodox Church and the Anglican Church also think of themselves as Catholic.)

The body of the two-volume work consists, then, of a highly sophisticated study of the creeds of Roman Catholicism and Protestantism, and of the history of Christianity, so far as either was known in this period at the very beginning of "the higher criticism." Having exhausted all local sources of information, the "I" of the book, who is represented as a student at Trinity College, then journeys to Germany, home of the rationalizing Protestant [Lutheran] theologians, to learn from professors of divinity in the German universities the basis of their views.

His findings and conclusions are embodied in letters to a woman friend in Ireland, whom, it seems, he was contemplating marrying if they could reconcile their religious opinions; one gathers that she must be a Protestant. He reports to her not only the lectures he attends but the contents of the books he studies. It is a clumsy and not very successful attempt to give human interest to what is essentially an intellectual discussion.

The *Travels* displays much erudition and real scholarship, but Moore's weakness for pedantry betrays him into a swampland of minutiae in which the reader is frequently bogged down. Exhaustive studies of the Church Fathers, and carefully recorded particulars of theological argument, do not make for easy reading. Very occasionally emotion breaks through the arid discussion: "There were moments when such a flood of religious feeling came over my heart as would not suffer any baser thoughts to live in their current." [8]

As might have been expected, the "Irish Gentleman" decides in the end to remain in the church of his fathers. His boasted neutrality soon gives way to his original bias. Moore was always a feeler more than a thinker, and the rationalistic element in Protestantism (particularly the German professors' severely reasoned theological system) antagonized him. "The Protestants' creed of . . . license of private judgment . . . attempts to bring down the grand and awful wonders of Christianity to the level of their own finite and low-thoughted reason." [9] Luther he calls bluntly a "blasphemer."

Undoubtedly Moore's innermost feelings as well as his critical mind were engaged in this work. "At last I found myself safe landed on Irish ground, and a far better Catholic than when I left it. . . . Reason is, in all heavenly things, a rash and ruinous guide." [10]

However, Moore must not be too closely identified with the "Irish Gentleman." *He* did not, for one thing, become "a better Catholic." The spokesman of the "Search" in the end did not marry his Protestant correspondent; whereas Moore married Bessy in a Protestant church, reared his children as Protestants, and was buried in a Protestant churchyard. The book must be considered rather as an attempt to voice what he believed would be the most probable reactions of educated, intellectual Irishmen to their emancipation from the disabilities which had previously affected them. Ironically, many wavering Roman Catholics must have been reconfirmed in their faith by this book, written by a man who himself (though always thinking of himself as a believing

Catholic) followed the requirements of that church most indiffer-
ently.

IV   The Epicurean

Both *Captain Rock* and the *Travels of an Irish Gentleman,* despite the emotionalism of the one and the sometimes deadly pedantry of the other, are distinguished by a lucidity that is one of
Moore's most attractive attributes as a prose writer. *The Epicurean,* unfortunately, is not. Moore failed with it in prose, as he had
failed with it (as *Alciphron*) in verse.

Lalla Rookh was sufficient evidence of how muddled his knowledge of the Near East really was, and *The Epicurean* com-
pounded that demonstration. He had, to begin with, no talent for
fiction; he could depict a personality pungently (for example,
Fadladeen in *Lalla Rookh* and even his characterization of the
mythical Captain Rock), but he could not probe psychologically a
character he had imagined, or make a story move consistently to a
logical conclusion.

As in the unfinished poem, so in the prose narrative, a young
disciple of the Epicurean philosophy goes to Egypt from Greece
to study theology—much as the "Irish Gentleman" went to Germany from Ireland. Moore knew a good deal about the literature
of ancient Greece, but he knew very little about Egypt, and less
than that about the old Egyptian religion—which he portrays as
still existent in Roman times, many centuries after it had faded
away. Moreover, though he had a scholar's and translator's knowledge of Greek history, he had less of Greek philosophy of the
great age, and his view of Epicureanism is superficial and inaccurate.

The young hierophant's principal reason for his journey is his
hope of learning the secret of immortality, which he thinks may
be in the possession of the mystics and philosophers of the more
ancient land. Instead, being a creation of Thomas Moore's, he
meets a young Egyptian priestess, Alethe, who is a crypto-convert
to Christianity. Through her influence he in turn is converted by
the hermit monks of the Thebaid. At the end of the book he dies a
martyr under Valerian—who had nothing to do with Egypt and is
not known as a persecutor of the early Christians.

What little life there is in this peculiar seminovel appears in its attacks on priestcraft (Egyptian priestcraft, not Christian). He is still incurably the son of the anticlerical John Moore. Aside from this, *The Epicurean* is little more than another of the innumerable pious tracts of its time cast in the mould of fiction. George Saintsbury dismissed it mildly as "a not unremarkable example of ornate prose." [11]

Not unexpectedly, it was extremely popular, and was read with avidity by thousands who reveled in its exotic background with no regard for its philosophical arguments and no interest in its ludicrous inaccuracies. This at least was one book by Thomas Moore which mothers could permit their young daughters to read! Only the perspicacious Thomas Love Peacock pointed out, in *The Westminster Review*, its gross anachronisms and historical errors. Edition after edition came out, and the one in 1839 was glorified by illustrations by no less a personage than J. M. W. Turner. (This was the edition which bore as an appendix the uncompleted poem, *Alciphron*, from which *The Epicurean* sprang.) When, in 1900, Rider Haggard's *She* appeared, he was accused of having plagiarized Moore's book! There is not the slightest resemblance between them—and Haggard, though otherwise a far lesser author, was at least innocent of what Howard Mumford Jones called Moore's "verbalism and sonorous general nouns."

Besides these three major nonbiographical prose works, Moore wrote other minor prose articles or pamphlets. Most notable is his *Letter to the Roman Catholics of Dublin,* in 1810, which dealt with the claim of the English Parliament to veto the rulings of Irish bishops as they did of English ones. It had dignity and force —but no effect upon Parliament.

There are other existent examples of satirical and polemic prose by Moore, but perhaps his most curious book is one that is no longer extant. That is the early (1806) *Sketches of Pious Women* —a series of amatory prose expositions followed by verse translations of devotional writings by the Latin Church Fathers. There are twenty-two of the "pious women," starting with Mary Magdalene—and the twenty-second is decidedly *not* from the Church Fathers, for it deals with the mythical "Pope Joan." The nature of Moore's expositions may be guessed from the fact that later, when he was trying to live down his early reputation as a writer of erotica, he paid a substantial sum to his then publisher, James Carpenter, to suppress the book, which hence is unobtainable. It is probably just as well for Moore's present prestige.

V *The Journal*

No survey of Thomas Moore's prose writings is complete without consideration of his published *Memoirs, Journal, and Correspondence*. The greatest part of these eight volumes (nearly 2900 pages) consists of excerpts from his diaries, which he kept faithfully through his years of activity, and which constituted his very last fragmentary output before his ability to write failed him altogether.

As we have seen, Moore always anticipated publication of his private journal after his death. In his will, he put the responsibility for editing the material on his friend, Lord John Russell. When Moore died, Russell was the British Prime Minister. He had little leisure for such a task, and little aptitude for it. He had written several political histories and biographies, as well as essays, stories, and plays, but his editorial experience was purely in his own field of politics. The material turned over to him was overwhelming, and might well have daunted an editor able to give all his working time to it. But he was devoted to Moore, and he shouldered the responsibility as best he could. It was four years after Moore's death before the final volume was published. The result was not entirely satisfactory, but that was Moore's own fault for laying such a burden on a man unable to give it his whole attention. An abbreviated volume of selections from the journals (the letters are of little importance; Moore was not noted as a letter-writer), such as the one made by J. B. Priestley, is still readable; the full eight volumes are not.

In his first preface (there were two), Russell said that he felt Moore's genius to have been "so remarkable that the world ought to be acquainted with the daily current of his life." To which Richard Henry Stoddard, in a rather ill-natured Introduction to his selections from the *Memoirs*, retorted that Moore was "the most voluminous and the most trivial of journalizers. . . . Moore had ceased to charm, and the details of his life were not cared for." [12] But even Stoddard, who thought the journal "obsolete," acknowledged that he found in it a "freshness and sparkle" that he did not find in Moore's poetry.

The admiring Russell is obliged to concede that in his journal Moore "seldom notices the instructive portion of the conversations" he had held with the eminent. That is more or less true: Coleridge's confusion befuddled him, Wordsworth's pomposity annoyed him, and he never took Lamb seriously. Yet he was most generous in his tributes to what he could understand of Coleridge's long philosophical disquisitions, for example, and was ready to blame himself for being bored. He could not help feeling more comfortable in company where wit took the place of philosophy, and where he himself was the star. His personal reactions give us some vivid pictures that bring these great figures nearer to us than could a dutiful report of the "instructive portion" of their talk.

The journal runs from 1818 to 1847, when he lost his capacity to write. The *Memoirs* include also an unfinished autobiography which carries him only to 1799, when he was twenty. His only other autobiographical writing is in the prefaces to each of the ten volumes of the 1840 collected *Poetical Works*. There are also upward to four hundred letters in the *Memoirs*, but few of any biographical or literary value. The lasting importance of all this huge mass of material lies in the journal itself, which was a genuine day-to-day account of his doings, of his writing, and often of his thoughts and feelings.

True, the journal is too facile and too superficial. The mere fact that Moore intended it for publication keeps it from being too intimate. It deals far more with his daily comings and goings, the people he met—and particularly what they had to say about him —and with current political events, than it does even with his work as an author. There is, however, a great deal of information to be gleaned of his literary methods and progress, and of his critical judgment of his own work as well as of the work of others. Where occasionally the journal does become really personal, it touches the heart; his description of his daughter Anastasia's death is still painful to read. The journal does in the end give us an all-over picture of the man himself, and in Moore's case the man was very much the father of the author. As L. A. G. Strong says, the journal with all its failings and deficiencies is "easy, flexible, and unaffected." [13]

J. B. Priestley, in his one-volume selections from the journal, notes that Moore in his diaries "presents the picture of an age," and points out that he was "not only *in* but *of* the Regency," and must be judged from the viewpoint of his era, as "an Englishman's idea of what an Irishman should be." [14]

Having always at the back of his mind the thought that some day his private words would become public, subconsciously if not consciously Moore built up in his journal the image he wished to present to posterity. He never doubted that posterity would cherish the image.

Much of the journal is merely good racy gossip, retailed with penetration and irony. Because his social world contained so many whose names now are far better known than his own, this is valuable biographical material. His account of his visit to Sir Walter Scott at Abbotsford, for instance, is a little masterpiece. And that he did not miss the irony of his welcome in that Tory household is evidenced by some verses he confided to his diary and called "Thoughts on Editors." John Lockhart, Scott's son-in-law, as editor of *Blackwood's Magazine*, had criticized Moore's writing viciously; as host to the visitor, he was the soul of hospitality. Moore remarked plaintively:

> No, editors don't care a button
> What false and faithless things they do.
> They'll let you come and cut their mutton,
> And then they'll have a cut at you.[15]

Of course the journal displays often Moore's innocent vanity; but it was a vanity that concealed a deep self-doubt. If his head had been turned at all by the flattery he received, it had long ago come back to a sensible balance. He speaks of "tributes which I feel the more gratified by from an inward consciousness that I but little deserve them. Yet this is what to the world appears vanity." [16] He would have been a fool not to have realized how famous he was.

If there is much in the journal about money and publishers' contracts and copyrights, it is because Moore was not, like many of his friends, a rich man writing for pleasure or fame, but a professional who earned his living by his pen. Wordsworth told him that up to 1835 (when he was sixty-five) he had received not more than £1000 for all his poems. "I dare say," wrote Moore, "that I have made by my writings at least twenty times that sum; but then I have written twenty times as much, such as it is." [17] And again: "For poor devils like me to fag and to be pinched for means becomes, as it were, second nature." [18]

In the face of this, can one blame him for heartening himself against self-doubt, for mentioning that Scott "spoke of my happy power of adopting words to music, which, he said, he could never attain, nor could Byron either";[19] or for remembering how Coleridge "spoke eloquently of the perfect union . . . of poetry and music" in the *Irish Melodies*? [20] That, after all, *was* his particular gift.

That Moore did not overestimate himself may be seen in his anxious query to Mary Shelley whether her husband had really liked his poems. (And this at a time when relatively few would have considered either Coleridge or Shelley one whose approval was of importance.) Moore copied into his journal her comforting words: "Be assured that as genius is the best judge of genius, those poems of yours which you yourself would value most were admired by *none* so much as Shelley." Only true humility would have felt the need for such reassurance from others.

Without Moore's background of literary achievement, his journal would in itself have little interest for us, and would indeed never have been published. It is because, as Priestley remarks, Moore was in his day "after Scott and Byron the most successful man of letters of his time" that anyone concerned with either the writer or the literary scene must still have recourse to this "picture of an age, . . . catching history as it flies." [21] For, Priestley adds, Moore "did not make his life serve his diary, but simply made his diary mirror his life." [22] Peter Quennell says much the same: one "cannot pretend that Moore deserves to rank with the great journal writers of the 19th century . . . His object was to produce a daily record of sayings and doings, not a detailed self-portrait, yet a remarkable self-portrait certainly emerges." [23] What is true of the journal is also true of Moore's letters. Commenting on Wilfrid S. Dowden's edition of the letters, Raymond Mortimer remarks: "They display his worries and his warmth of heart more often than his wit." [24]

CHAPTER 8

The Man of Letters and
the Creative Artist: Summation

I The Scholar and Critic

THE old-fashioned term "man of letters" or "litterateur" best describes Thomas Moore in one aspect, but only in one. Had he himself been asked, he would undoubtedly have described himself as a poet, since "the commencement of my career in rhyming was so very early as to be almost beyond the reach of memory." He also said, "My pen has been my sole support" (not exactly true, but approximating the truth: he would not have received the Bermuda appointment, his only other source of income, had he not been a recognized writer whom his influential friends wished to help); and at no time in history have most writers been able to earn a living entirely through the writing of poetry. Moore disliked to do hack work ("I hate Albumising, Annualising, and Periodicalising")—as what creative writer does not? Yet it is fortunate for him that when necessity drove him he was able to function as a hack, if a glorified one, and even to turn some of his assigned tasks into literary productions in their own right.

He declined offers to edit both *The Edinburgh Review* and *The Times,* and he always refused to contribute to the then popular Annuals.[1] But he seldom refused an offer of a book contract—the proposed biography of Canning is the only one on record—and even when the task was onerous or quite beyond him he felt obliged to take it on; the *History of Ireland* is a prime example. Indeed, it may be said that many of his series of songs, after the earlier volumes of the *Irish Melodies,* were written to order and under obligation instead of being the spontaneous results of inspiration.

In another sense also Moore was a man of letters: he was something of a savant, a little of a scholar, and a good deal of a pedant. His erudition was real. His education had been the narrow but thorough classical one of his time, and he had a scholar's knowledge of Greek and Latin, besides a working knowledge of French and Italian and probably some slight acquaintance with German. He is reputed to have published a complete translation of the Roman historian Sallust in 1807, but if so it must have appeared anonymously and has been lost. His so-called translations from the supposed odes of Anacreon, from the Greek Anthology, and from Catullus, Propertius, and Tibullus are free versions rather than exact translations; but they could not have been written had he not been steeped in their original languages. Except in the songs, Moore is essentially a bookish writer; his work smells of the library and the lamp. He was familiar, perhaps too familiar, with many recondite authors; as Howard Mumford Jones says, " 'Odd, out-of-the-way reading' . . . clutters too much of his printed work." [2]

We must always remember how essentially he belonged to his own age. It was an age of snobbish pedantry, when the bookish author was the admired author. The writer's audience was presumed to be made up entirely of readers as well educated and as cultured as himself. Moore had little love for avowedly "popular" writing—most of which in his time as in ours was trash. He remarks in his journal: "Broached . . . my notions (long entertained by me) respecting the ruinous effects on literature likely to arise from the boasted diffusion of education; the lowering of the standard that must necessarily arise from the extending of the circle of judges. . . . Most will write down to the lowered standards. All the great things in literature have been achieved when the readers were few." [3] That sounds rather shocking to us, but it did not sound so to Moore or to his readers.

On the whole he was pessimistic about the prospects of English literature, particularly of poetry. He "doubted much the power of any poem to make an impression on the public, dosed as they have been with rhymes." He was not a prophet, and he could not foresee the great poets of the later nineteenth century. Even poetry, he felt, could only be degraded by appealing to too wide a public. When Sir James Mackintosh declared that "the best art pleased the greatest number of people," Moore dissented—even though Mackintosh's examples were Homer and Shakespeare. He thought that statement might be true of "such a sensual art as music," but not of poetry, "for the enjoyment of which knowledge is necessary." [4]

Despite these limitations, Moore was not a bad critic. He was hampered by these preconceived ideas of literary excellence, but for work that fell within them he had an acute and perceptive eye. He recognized the greatness of Shelley when few did; he respected Wordsworth as a poet; he saw Byron's defects as well as his splendors. As Lord Russell said: "he had a good opinion of his own powers and was delighted with every tribute, . . . but his love of praise was united with the most generous and liberal dispensation of praise to others." [5] W. F. Trench rightly called him "a critic whose judgment contrasts to his advantage with the judgment of his greater contemporaries." [6]

Judging Moore as a scholar, one must not forget also his masterly technique and his bold metrical experiments. Moore began to write poetry in a period of aridity, a sort of poetic gap between the eighteenth-century Augustan Poets and the early nineteenth-century Romantics. Because Moore was a contemporary of the Romantic Poets, we tend to forget that he antedated them in publication. The *Odes of Anacreon,* which first brought him fame, appeared in 1800. Byron was then twelve years old, Keats five, and Shelley four. They all died long before him, but he was much their senior. The Lake Poets were all older than Moore, and published earlier—Wordsworth's and Coleridge's *Lyrical Ballads,* which became the rallying-cry of the "new poetry," came out in 1798; but though their final influence was immense, the attention they attracted at the time was almost nil. As Jones notes, Moore possessed technical resources of the first rank; for "sheer craftsmanship" he was on a level with Coleridge, Keats, Shelley, and Poe, and better equipped than either Wordsworth or Byron. In this regard he was not surpassed until the arrival of Tennyson and Browning.

Purely as a man of letters he earned and received the esteem of competent critics. "Consummate" was Richard Garnett's word for him in this respect. And he had a peculiar distinction, in that he was "the first Irish man of letters to be identified with his country." [7] The sole dissent to this dictum comes from William F. P.

Stockley, who complains sourly that "by his popular English works, he helped forward, in a country then chiefly Gaelic-speaking, the . . . neglect of the Irish language; . . . he helped to turn the Irish into imitators of another country." [8] However, even this is in a way a back-handed compliment.

II *The Creative Writer*

Much as Moore was esteemed in his own lifetime as litterateur, critic, and scholar, if he is to be a surviving literary figure at all, he must be judged basically as a creative writer. And as a creative writer he must be judged primarily as a lyric poet. Much of his satire was too topical to be alive today, and his narrative poems are not in the fashion of our times.

As for his prose, *Captain Rock* died with the cause it advocated, and is only of historical interest today. The *Travels of an Irish Gentleman in Search of a Religion* would probably be read voluntarily now only by those looking for light on religious doubt, of a highly specialized variety. *The Epicurean* and the *History of Ireland* are better forgotten—and are forgotten.

There remain the three biographies. Only a student of Irish history, again, would find it worth his while to seek out the life of Lord Edward Fitzgerald. The biography of Sheridan is in a different category; it is still a useful source-book, though not an impeccable one; and no one concerned with dramatic history can afford to ignore it: but it was one of the works which Moore did more for money than for love, and it shows the effects. The life of Byron is by far the best and the most living of Moore's prose writing. It is a "standard" biography, a minor classic, and if only because Byron himself was so brilliant a journalist and letter-writer, and because Moore knew him so intimately and understood him so well, it is still eminently readable.

Moore as a writer, however, must stand and fall by his "songs, set to music," and his other lyrical poems and passages in poems. They have had their denigrators as well as their adulators; but the point is that they have deserved both. The best of them, as Horace with better reason said of his own poems, will not "wholly die."

Moore's failings as a lyric poet are patent. They are sentimentality and superficiality. About the sentimentality we can do nothing;

it was the weakness of the period in which he wrote and of a long time after. The superficiality, however, is sometimes more apparent than real.

Moore is always accused of being too facile. True, his verse came easily, but it was not slipshod; he did not present it to the world just as it first bubbled up from his inner depths. He was an indefatigable worker, who labored over his poems and polished them. Stephen Gwynn remarks: "He helped on the extraordinary advance in poetical technique which marks the years from 1795 to the rise of Tennyson. Moore's sense of style is always faulty. . . . But he had a fine ear for meter." [9] And as "an artist in meter," he goes on to say, Moore is still important. Shallow Moore may often have been, but his songs, even without their music, are "more varied, more truly lyrical, . . . more soundly built than careless reading shows." [10]

One of Moore's great defects is that, as J. B. Priestley put it, "he starves our visual sense." That is to say, his writing is remarkably bare of description, either of nature or of persons; he was interested in the bent of mind and the turn of feeling, but not in outward appearance. He himself said that imagination can "best describe what it has not seen." And when he does essay to depict the object of his fancy, it is always in the most general terms and the most obvious clichés. A lovely girl always has rosy cheeks and a white neck and shining hair, and she is always quite indistinguishable from every other pretty girl. And you will search Moore in vain to find any sharp picture of a mountain or a river or a forest, even in that verse travelogue, *Rhymes for the Road.*

This leads directly to another of his weaknesses, his hopeless confusion of imagination and fancy. Once synonymous, these words have long ago become differentiated. Fancy is the lesser thing: it is passive and superficial and deals with random associations. Imagination is active and creative and in its full glory is the surest attribute of literary genius. To Moore, there was no distinction between them. In consequence (to the modern reader at least) there is something capricious and strained about Moore's flights of fancy, which seldom delve deep or soar high.

This is not to say that Moore *never* achieved depths or heights. Poe had a word to say about that. "Fancy so far predominates over all his other faculties and over the fancy of all other men as to have induced . . . the idea that he is fanciful only. . . . Never was a grosser wrong done the fame of a true poet." [11]

As an example, he adduces Moore's song, "I Would I Were by That Dim Lake," of which he says that "no poem is more profoundly more *weirdly* imaginative." (Another of which this could be said is "Oh, Ye Dead!") But then Poe, though a better poet and a better critic than Moore, himself does not always distinguish carefully between imagination and fancy.

Fancy, and worse, fancifulness, was one of the besetting sins of the verse of the early nineteenth century. The end result was to bore the bewildered reader. Moore himself perceived this, and it may have been one factor in his gradual abandonment of verse for prose. (He was quite well aware that, as Gwynn says, his later poetry was "little more than fluent verse.") He himself had not contributed to this satiation of the reading public; he was saved by his craftsmanship and by his fidelity to the musical standards he had set himself; but his followers and imitators had no such safe-guards.

In the *Irish Melodies* most of all, he was able so to fit the Gaelic rhythm, and even peculiarities of ancient Irish poetry such as its dependence on assonance, to the old airs that he produced "a wholly new and beautiful effect." He knew no Gaelic; but he did know music, and he had the true lyrical gift. Yet fundamentally, to him "poetry was the language of fancy, not of fact. It existed, ornamentally, at a remove from life." [12] He asked, in his journal: "Where do all the imaginary scenes . . . go, if it is necessary to see what we describe in order to be a true poet?" [13] That sentence is in a sense Moore's poetic credo—and to some degree also it must serve as an indictment.

III *Influences on and by Moore*

Moore absorbed easily the pervading atmosphere, but for that very reason there were few direct influences on him as a writer. In other words, in both verse and prose he wrote in the idiom of his time, and just because that came so automatically to him, individual writers with an original idiom of their own had little to say to him. To hypothesize an example, he would have been quite unable (as well as unwilling) to imitate the pastoral simplicity of the *Lyrical Ballads.* Unlike Wordsworth's "Peter Bell," "a primrose by a river's brim" most decidedly was not, to him, a yellow primrose and "nothing more"; his primrose would have been transmogrified into a flower reminiscent of exotic associations (duly annotated in a footnote), and, moreover, viewed through a mist of sentimental tears.

The only poetic influence he acknowledged was, oddly enough, that of Alexander Pope. The early satirical poems, *Corruption, Intolerance,* and *The Sceptic,* he openly avowed to have been written in imitation of Pope's *Essay on Man* and *Essay on Criticism.* They were Moore's last tribute to the spirit of the eighteenth century—unless we can instance his continued use of the rhymed couplets in iambic pentameter which were the favorite verse-form of the Augustan Poets.

It may be asked: what of the influence on Moore of the ancient bardic songs of the Irish harpers, the source of all the *Irish Melodies?* The answer is that there was none; if any words survived to these airs, Moore, knowing no Gaelic, would have been unable to read them. This may have been what Richard Garnett had in mind when he said that there was "little specifically Celtic in [Moore's] genius except his wit and animation" [14]—though Garnett goes on to deplore Moore's lack of Matthew Arnold's "Celtic Magic," which makes little sense since Arnold was not a Celt.

Garnett also called Moore "a brilliant satellite of Byron," but here again he is in error. If his narrative poems, and particularly *Lalla Rookh,* remind us of Byron, it is not because Byron's style had influenced Moore's, but because they both gravitated toward subjects, such as the Near East and its "mystery" and "romance," which were popular at the time. Moore was a published poet long before Byron. And Byron certainly never thought of Moore as a "satellite"; he regarded the older man as at least his equal in talent as well as in fame. If there was any influence either way, which in all probability there was not, it would have been that of Moore on Byron, not that of Byron on Moore.

In prose, also, except for the fact that Moore wrote in the standard fashion of his day—the chronologically arranged biographies, with their inclusion of uncut letters and journal entries; the multivolumed works full of painstaking detail—there is little evidence that any one particular writer had any important effect on Moore. He did say that his ideal as a biographer was to follow in the footsteps of James Boswell; but there is no hint of Boswell's style or method in even the best of Moore's biographies, that of Byron. As for the polemics in the Irish cause, notably *Captain Rock,* there was plenty of other writing in this same general vein, but decidedly none of it became a model for Moore. As a matter of fact, he disliked its approach and style heartily. Moore was never more an original than in his ironic prose and verse dealing with English domination of Ireland; and if occasionally he reaches almost the white-hot, searing incandescence of Jonathan Swift, it is not because of any specific influence on him of such works as *The Drapier Letters* or the *Modest Proposal,* as because the same wrongs had drawn from him the same burning resentment and cutting satire.

Similarly, Moore had little specific influence on those who came after him. He had a host of imitators, but none worth serious consideration. It was a period of artificial sentimental verse, and much that looks like a debt to Moore is really only a debt to the popular mode.

In one respect Moore might well have influenced later poets, and that was in his masterly technique. But there is no one person to whom one can point with confidence as having gone to school to Moore and consciously followed his cunning craftsmanship. Moore was a pioneer of modern metrics, but not a teacher.

IV *The Critical Consensus*

Strictly speaking, there never has been a critical consensus on the writings of Thomas Moore. In his lifetime he was the recipient of hysterical praise, for half a century afterward he was fondly remembered, then he was either completely neglected or made the butt of ridicule and contempt; and only after all that did the few who considered him at all endeavor in the light of modern standards of criticism to make a reasonable and just evaluation of his work. The severest censure he has received has not been put into words; it is the silent evidence of forgetfulness, the disappearance of his name from serious criticism and of his books from the interest of readers.

In 1834 the *Dublin Evening Mail* predicted rashly that 'the poetry of the Irish Anacreon is imperishable while there exists a heart to beat with love, or pant with patriotism"—a verdict worthy of Moore himself in his most maudlin mood. This kind of idolatry was not confined to such parochial commentators. It was Byron who said: "Moore has a peculiarity of talent all his own, which never was, nor will be, possessed by another. There is nothing Moore may not do, if he will but seriously set about it." It was Shelley who in *Adonais* coupled Moore with Byron in one stanza:

> From her wilds Ierne sent
> The sweetest lyrist of her saddest wrong,
> And love taught grief to fall like music from his tongue.

Hailed as an equal by such voices, it is a marvel that Moore could sigh in his journal that he had never "been much in repute with certain great guns of Parnassus." Neither is it surprising that he saw nothing incongruous in aspiring to immortality as one of the great of English poetry. To his contemporaries he *was* in that rank; in 1858 Lord Russell could write seriously: "Of English lyrical poets, Moore is surely the greatest"—a statement which seems to us absurd, but which went unchallenged when it was made.

Even in Moore's own time, however, there were not lacking critics to take a less extravagant view. Moore noted in his journal a rather odd but significant dictum uttered by Francis Jeffrey in 1844, to the effect that the fame of current poets had fluctuated badly in their own lifetime: "Rogers and Campbell [15] are without the least mark of decay," while Keats, Shelley, Byron, and Wordsworth were becoming forgotten, "and even the splendid strains of Moore are fading into distance and dimness, except where they have been married to immortal music." [16] The wheel of time has turned again: Keats, Shelley, Byron, and Wordsworth have recovered their glory, whereas Moore is forgotten with Rogers and Campbell. Leigh Hunt also proved to be a poor prophet: "His [Moore's] sort of talent has this advantage in it, that being of a description intelligible to all, the possessor is equally sure of present and future fame." The most acute critic of Moore in his own time was William Hazlitt—who was also the greatest English literary critic of his day. Hazlitt was a bit prejudiced against Moore for political reasons; nevertheless, his summing up is as level-headed as it is witty: "His verse is like a shower of beauty; a dance of imagery; a stream of music; . . . a continuous and incessant flow of voluptuous thoughts and shining allusions. . . . He ought to write with a crystal pen on silver paper. . . . Sooner than not stimulate or delight, he is willing to be tawdry, or artificial, or commonplace. . . . He seduces the taste and enervates the imagination. . . . A play of fancy, a glitter of words, a shallowness of thought." [17] This is very much the same thing as Howard Mumford Jones meant when he said that Moore "restored music to English verse," but that too often "the sense is drowned in sound." [18]

The Victorian critics assessed Moore still seriously, but more soberly. George Saintsbury said that he "ranks with those poets who have expressed easily and acceptably the thoughts and fancies of the average man. . . . His note of feeling, if not strong or deep, is true and real. His faculty of expression is not only considerable, but it is also distinguished." [19] This is really damning with faint praise; and Richard Garnett strikes the same note of slight condescension. He agrees that Moore is "an inexhaustible fount of melody," but makes it plain that Moore possessed talent, not genius. The best he can say in the way of grudging encomium is that Moore is among "poets of the library, who embalm the spirit of their own age and hand its volatile essence down to posterity in a compact and clarified form." [20] This is a harsh but perspicacious judgment, and it comes close to the most definitive evaluation of Moore, by a late nineteenth-century critic—the Frenchman Louis Cazamian: "Literary history will probably leave him one of the first rank among the Romanticists of the second order: for his poetry, however nerveless it may be, possesses an element of inspired originality in its music and flow and the felicity of its language." [21]

Even as late as 1905 Stephen Gwynn could call Moore "still one of the most popular and widely known [poets] throughout the English-speaking world." [22] Twenty years later that was no longer so; soldiers did not sing the songs from the *Irish Melodies* in World War I as they did in the American Civil War. There came then a period in which Moore's name was still faintly remembered in English-speaking countries. It was marked by appearance of the two best modern biographies, those by L.A.G. Strong and Howard Mumford Jones. These books, however, were published some thirty years ago, and today Moore is almost completely forgotten, outside of his native land at least. Dublin has a Moore Society, there is the statue "facing the bank of Ireland" and a monument of sorts in the Vale of Avoca; and doubtless there are other societies and other remembrances. But the Ireland of which Thomas Moore was the "Voice" is not twentieth century Eire, and it may be doubted whether anybody there under the age of sixty still considers Moore a major poet. Even the centenary of his death, in 1952, elicited only one notice in a general magazine, that by Denzil England; and that could hardly be called a tribute when it speaks of "verses . . . enormously popular in the first half of the last century, but which strike us as a little too stilted and having been once a little too scented, though bearing now the faintly musty aroma comes upon things for a time all too fashionable." [23]

Other recent commentators have been still more cruel. Ralph Hodgson, who was kinder to animals than he was to human beings, sneered: "Comes a rather female song,/Sweet and sad: 'tis Tommy Moore." Another *fin de siècle* English poet was even more brutal—and betrayed an utter ignorance of what either Moore or his writing was like. When Yeats omitted anything by Lord Alfred Douglas from *The Oxford Book of Modern Verse* which he was editing, Douglas telegraphed angrily that Yeats's act was "typical of the attitude of the minor poet to the major one. Had Thomas Moore been editing such a book he would have omitted Keats and Shelley." [24] This is ridiculously unfair and untrue: had Moore been editing such an anthology he would most certainly have included Shelley, and doubtless Keats too if someone had suggested him. (He does not seem to have known Keats's poetry at all, since he never mentions him.)

Moore's two major modern biographers are temperate and discerning. I have quoted frequently the appraisals by Howard Mumford Jones, whose *The Harp That Once*— is indubitably the best biography of Moore. In *The Minstrel Boy*, L.A.G. Strong is equally judicious in his evaluations. "One particular job," he points out, "on the borderline between poetry and music, he did as well as it has ever been done. . . . For general ideas he had little aptitude. He romanticized them, made them personal, or turned them into a safety valve, an outlet for his Irish combativeness. . . . His poetry lacks subtlety and depth of imagination. It comes rather from fancy, . . . gentle, after-dinner melancholy, and a dexterous lightness." [25]

This pretty well sums up Moore as a poet, and sees him whole. Wyn J. Tucker concerns himself primarily with Moore as an Irish writer. "With Thomas Moore the poetry of modern Ireland begins." This is too large a claim: Moore is hardly recognizable as a forerunner of Yeats, for example. It is true, however, that Moore was the first to sing of Ireland in English tones, to write widely read poetry written in English on Irish themes. Tucker does not contend that Moore was in any sense a great poet; he knows the poetry is prevailingly unoriginal, often commonplace and conventional. But he asks us not to begrudge Moore a modest place on Parnassus: "The graceful, tender [verse] . . . in which Moore excels reveals simple tenderness of feeling expressed in the simplest language, without aiming at imagery. . . . [If his lyrics] do not transport you to 'a peak in Darien,' they conduct you through very agreeable meadowland." [26]

All this is certainly true of the songs, and especially of the *Irish Melodies*. In the longer poems, particularly the narrative poems, the very lucidity, simplicity, and grace become a handicap to the modern reader, accustomed as he is to more involved and cerebral poetry. Peter Quennell says it better: "To a modern ear [Moore's verses] sound somewhat slight and sugary, . . . [but] the emotion that inspired the songs, though not deep, was certainly clear." [27] Quennell makes the interesting suggestion that Moore did for Ireland what Theocritus did for Sicily by bringing into English literature for the first time the legends and the poetic spirit of his native Ireland.

V *Final Summation*

It is in the *Irish Melodies* that Moore comes closest to greatness and to true originality. It is of them that Seamus McCall is thinking when he predicts: "It may well be that the exuberant style, the vigorous coloring, the disciplined form, and the musical lyric of which Moore was the master will again return to favor." [28]

It is not likely, at least in the near future. We are nearer in spirit to both the seventeenth and the eighteenth centuries than we are to the nineteenth—to Donne and Marvell, or Pope and Dryden, than to Byron or Wordsworth (or, for that matter, Tennyson or

Browning). Our poetry has lost its melody and become increasingly intellectual. This too is a fashion that will pass, as all fashions do; but it is improbable that we shall then revert to *Lalla Rookh* or *The Loves of the Angels* as our models, or even to the *Irish Melodies*. We are too cynical to weep, too despairing to burst into generous anger, far too sophisticated for sentimentality or even open sentiment. Thomas Moore is a poet of yesterday, not of today or tomorrow. Yet he will not be altogether lost to sight. There may never again be many to cherish him, but there will always be a few susceptible to the music of his Irish harp—and they will not all be Irish.

As a man of letters he is dated beyond resurrection. As a biographer he will be remembered for the Byron alone, and that mainly as a first-hand source for researchers. Most of his vigorous and pungent satire has perished with the wrongs that aroused it. His full *Journal* is far too voluminous for the patience of modern readers; engaging as its revelation is of a human being who, for all his foibles, is both admirable and endearing, we owe a debt of gratitude to J. B. Priestley for having cut it down to manageable size. Lalla Rookh, the semi-Oriental bride, has become a silly bore; and the love affairs of fallen angels no longer attract us. "Not a great poet," we say, "nor a great man." And we shut the volume.

But there remain still those faint, sweet strains, almost drowned in the flood of affectation and ornamentation, but still clear, simple, and moving. For the sake of those few poignant lyrics, if for nothing else, Thomas Moore should not be forever neglected and forgotten: nor will he be.

In sum, then, we have in him a man almost ruined by quick fame beyond his deserts, followed inevitably by too great a reversal of opinion. From the residue we may pluck a few fragments which serve to show us that our ancestors were not entirely fools when they chose him to be one of the most overwhelmingly admired authors of his own day.

Notes and References

Chapter One

1. Pronounced "Moor" in Ireland, "More" in England.
2. *The Minstrel Boy,* by L. A. G. Strong, p. 4.
3. William Hazlitt, "Mr. Thomas Moore and Mr. Leigh Hunt," in *The Spirit of the Age,* p. 359 of 1825 edition.
4. Howard Mumford Jones, *The Harp That Once—,* p. 20.
5. Paraphrased from *Essays in Irish Biography,* by William F. P. Stockley.
6. In 1804 Moore was calling the Americans "rabble." By 1816 he confessed that "my sentiments in respect to their national and individual characters are much changed."
7. Doris Langley Moore noted in *The Atlantic Monthly,* August, 1959, that Moore's "overdelicate deference" in the Memoir-burning affair was due to "the kind of defensive pride which is found chiefly in men who lack security."
8. In 1831 Moore remarked in his Journal that Sydney Smith had asked him how he "felt about dying." He added: "I answered that if my mind was but at ease about the comfort of those I left behind, I should leave the world without much regret."
9. Like all Moore's homes, it was rented; he never owned a house. Lansdowne's library was outstanding; Joseph Priestley had once been its librarian.
10. According to her tombstone, she was sixty-eight and had been a child bride; according to her birth certificate she was eighty-three.
11. An Irish Member of Parliament wanted to know if Moore was to receive a pension for "making luscious ballads for lovesick maidens, or for writing lampoons upon George IV." To which *The Times* retorted that "the name of Thomas Moore is in itself a credit to the Pension List," and *The London Standard,* though it was a Tory organ, called the pension "a tribute to genius—a testimony to the claims of one who, if not the first living poet, is certainly not second to any with whom the present generation has lived."
12. Stockley, *op. cit.*

13. Personal letter from the Reverend Mr. James Collins, until recently vicar of Bronham; dated June 5, 1964.

14. Jones, *op. cit.*, p. 324.

Chapter Two

1. Strong, *op. cit.*, p. 121.

2. Strong, p. 32.

3. John A. Robinson, "Dear Harp of My Country," *Etude* (March, 1942).

4. Hazlitt, *op. cit.* Hazlitt was, as noted previously, a Tory, which may have had some effect on the nature of his animadversions; he was, however, a very keen and just critic in the purely literary field.

5. Richard Garnett, *Essays of an Ex-Librarian*, p. 209.

6. Graham Hough, in *New York Herald Tribune Book Week*, April 13, 1964.

7. Strong, p. 300.

8. Jones, *op. cit.*, p. 110.

9. Strong, p. 214. (Strong's *The Minstrel Boy* is especially valuable for its comments on this phase of Moore's work.)

10. George Saintsbury, *Essays in English Literature*, p. 193.

11. Stephen L. Gwynn, *Thomas Moore*, p. 22.

Chapter Three

1. Jones, *op. cit.*, p. 175.

2. Wordsworth, *The Prelude*, Book XI.

3. Jones, p. 171.

4. Strong, *op. cit.*, p. 169.

5. Saintsbury, *op. cit.*, pp. 185–86.

6. Gwynn, *op. cit.*, p. 96.

7. Jones, p. 171.

8. Gwynn, p. 176.

9. Unsigned article in *Allibone Dictionary of English Literature and British and American Authors* (Philadelphia, 1902 [1923 edition]); quoted from *Portfolio of a Man of the World*, author not given.

10. *Personal Reminiscences of Moore and Jerdan*, edited by Richard Henry Stoddard (New York, 1875). William Jerdan was a well-known critic and wit of his day (1782–1869).

Chapter Four

1. From 1812 to 1840, when Rowland Hill's postal reforms took place, postage charges were based on the distance the letter traveled. As it cost fourpence for fifteen miles, the Two-Penny Post must have

been local—another example of the topical allusions that were clear to Moore's contemporary readers if not to us.

2. The Holy Alliance was a declaration of principles signed in 1815, after the defeat of Napoleon at Waterloo, by Alexander I of Russia, Frederick William III of Prussia, and Francis I of Austria; it was followed by the less vague Grand Alliance. The object of both was to carve up Europe in the interest of the three dominant Continental powers, suppress the last traces of revolution in France, and in general clamp Europe in the grip of reaction. It was heartily approved by the English Tories, and as heartily excoriated by the Whigs.

3. Saintsbury, *op. cit.*, pp. 188–89.

4. John = England (John Bull); Sawney = Scotland; Paddy = Ireland.

5. Jones, *op. cit.*, p. 196.

6. ἐγώ δ' ὁ ΜΩΡΟΣ (*ego d' o MOROS*): "thus I, the fool"—"Moros" is meant as a facetious play upon "Moore." He couples this "confession" with that of authorship of the *Two-Penny Post-Bag* as well.

Chapter Five

1. Strong, *op. cit.*, p. 77.

2. *Edinburgh Review*, July, 1808.

3. From the "Odes to Nea."

4. The correct spelling is *Missolonghi*.

5. "Song," which begins, "Fly from the world, O Bessy, to me," was written long before Moore met Elizabeth Dyke, and is therefore not addressed to her.

Chapter Six

1. Warren Hastings was the first governor-general of British India; he was impeached for "high crimes and misdemeanors" in office, and exonerated only after seven years of trials. Sheridan was among his chief accusers in Parliament.

2. *Memoirs of the Life of the Right Honourable Richard Brinsley Sheridan*, 5th Edition, Vol. II, p. 464. (Further page references are made to "Sheridan," same edition.)

3. Sheridan, Vol. I, p. 245–46.

4. *Ibid.*, p. 141.

5. *Ibid.*, p. 143.

6. *Ibid.*, Vol. II, p. 463.

7. *Ibid.*, p. 475.

8. *Ibid.*, p. 486.

9. The "Ancient" is Marcus Antoninus.

10. Sheridan, Preface, p. v.

11. Moore's *Journal* (*Tom Moore's Diary*), pp. 127–28.

12. Doris Langley Moore, "The Burning of Byron's Memoirs," *The Atlantic Monthly* Vol. CCIV, No. 2 (August, 1959), pp. 27–37.

13. D. L. Moore, *The Late Lord Byron,* p. 138.

14. D. L. Moore, *op. cit.,* p. 29.

15. Jones, *op. cit.,* p. 276.

16. Garnett, *op. cit.,* p. 220.

17. D. L. Moore, *op. cit.,* p. 29.

18. In *Edinburgh Review,* June 18, 1830.

19. Strong, *op. cit.,* p. 234.

20. Jones, *op. cit.,* p. 273.

21. *Ibid.,* p. 276.

22. Strong, *op. cit.,* p. 235.

23. *Letters and Journals of Lord Byron,* 1932 edition, Vol. II, p. 661. (Further page references are made to "Byron," same edition.)

24. Byron, Vol. II, p. 643.

25. *Ibid.,* p. 655.

26. *The Life and Death of Lord Edward Fitzgerald,* 3rd edition, Vol. I, p. viii–ix. (Further page references are made to "Fitzgerald," same edition.)

27. Fitzgerald, Vol. II, p. 186.

28. Gwynn, *op. cit.,* p. 137.

29. Fitzgerald, Vol. II, p. 195.

30. *Ibid.,* Vol. I, p. 255.

Chapter Seven

1. Stockley, *op. cit.,* p. 8.

2. Ruth Lee Johnson, "The Voice of Ireland," *American Mercury,* 82 (January, 1956), p. 130.

3. Sydney Smith, Essays (London, 1873), p. 475.

4. *Ibid.,* p. 482.

5. *Memoirs of Captain Rock,* 3rd edition, p. 33.

6. Stockley, *op. cit.,* p. 16.

7. *Travels of an Irish Gentleman in Search of a Religion,* 1st edition, Vol. I, p. 2. (Further page references are made to "*Travels,*" same edition.)

8. *Travels,* Vol. I, p. 146.

9. *Ibid.,* Vol. II, pp. 207, 230.

10. *Ibid.,* pp. 238–39.

11. Saintsbury, *op. cit.,* p. 174.

12. *Personal Reminiscences of Moore and Jerdan,* p. xii. (Introduction by Richard Henry Stoddard.)

13. Strong, *op. cit.,* p. 286.

14. J. B. Priestley, in the Introduction to his condensation of the *Journal* (*Tom Moore's Diary*), p. vi, ix. Priestley says truly that the *Journal* is "far too prolix," and that it "gains from being compressed."

15. *Journal* (Priestley edition), pp. 184–85. (Further page references are made to "*Journal*," same edition.)

16. *Ibid.*, p. 162.

17. *Ibid.*, p. 208.

18. *Ibid.*, p. 80.

19. *Ibid.*, p. 177.

20. *Ibid.*, p. 206.

21. Priestley, Introduction, p. vi.

22. *Ibid.*, p. vii.

23. Peter Quennell, *Journal of Thomas Moore 1818–1841*, (New York, 1964), p. xiv.

24. (London) *Sunday Times*, February 14, 1965 (review of *The Letters of Thomas Moore*, edited by Wilfrid S. Dowden (London, 1964).

Chapter Eight

1. Annuals were a sort of miscellaneous illustrated book of essays, poems, and stories, usually brought out for the Christmas trade. The only modern semiapproximation to an Annual is *The Saturday Book* (published yearly in London by the Hutchinson Publishing Group).

2. Jones, *op. cit.*, p. 42.

3. *Journals*, p. 179.

4. *Ibid.*, p. 184.

5. *The Memoirs, Journals, and Correspondence of Thomas Moore*, edited by Lord John Russell, Vol. II, Preface.

6. *Tom Moore*, by W. F. Trench, Dublin, Three Candles Press, 1934.

7. Strong, *op. cit.*, p. 4.

8. Stockley, *op. cit.*, p. 3.

9. Gwynn, *op. cit.*, p. 122.

10. Jones, *op. cit.*, p. 111.

11. This passage is from Poe's essay, *The Poetic Principle*.

12. Strong, *op. cit.*, p. 342.

13. *Journal*, p. 39.

14. Garnett, *op. cit.*, p. 200.

15. Samuel Rogers (1763–1855) is now known chiefly as the host (his breakfasts were famous) of practically every celebrity of his time. Thomas Campbell (1777–1844), if remembered at all, is thought of as a critic and anthologist. In their own time both were considered poets of distinction.

16. *Journal,* p. 215. (And even the music itself is no longer "immortal.")

17. Hazlitt, *op. cit.,* p. 185.

18. Jones, *op. cit.,* p. 55.

19. Saintsbury, *op. cit.,* p. 199.

20. Garnett, *op. cit.,* p. 200, 255.

21. Quoted by W. M. Rossetti in the 1880 edition of Moore's poems, which he edited.

22. Gwynn, *op. cit.,* pp. 1–2.

23. *Contemporary Review,* Vol. xvii–xviii (March, 1952), pp. 157–62.

24. The telegram is quoted in *Bosie: Lord Alfred Douglas, His Friends and Enemies,* by Rupert Croft-Cooke (Indianapolis, 1963) p. 353.

25. Strong, *op. cit.,* p. 31, 107, 279, *seriatim.*

26. Wyn J. Tucker, "Literary Aspects of Ireland," *Catholic World,* Vol. CL, No. 900 (March, 1940), pp. 652–59.

27. Quennell, *op. cit.,* p. xv.

28. *Thomas Moore,* by MacCall Seamus, p. 7.

Selected Bibliography

PRIMARY SOURCES

THERE is no recent edition of Moore's collected verse and prose, and the latest volumes of his collected poems are also long out of print—evidence of his present neglect. A standard collection is the *Complete Poetical Work*, with a sketch by Nathan Haskell Dole (New York: T. Y. Crowell & Co., 1895). The latest available edition is *Poetical Works* (Boston: Cornhill Publishing Co., 1928).

Moore's poems, particularly the *Irish Melodies*, have been widely anthologized, and some of them can be found in all standard anthologies: *e.g., The Oxford Book of English Verse* (New York: Oxford University Press, 1948); *An Oxford Anthology of English Poetry*, edited by Howard Foster Lowry and Willard Thorp (New York: Oxford University Press, 1956); *Poems I Remember*, compiled by John Kieran, (Garden City, New York: Doubleday, Doran and Company, 1942); *The Golden Treasury of Songs and Lyrics*, edited by Francis T. Palgrave (New York: The Macmillan Company, 1937; *The Family Book of Best Loved Poems*, edited by David L. George (Garden City, New York: Hanover House, 1952).

The latest separate edition of *Lalla Rookh* is in the *Everyman's Library* (London: E. P. Dent & Co.; New York: E. P. Dutton & Co.): no date, but published in the 1930's.

The latest reprint of the *Life, Letters, and Journals of Lord Byron* (a revision of the original title) was brought out in London, by John Murray, in 1932. There are no modern reprints of the other biographies or the other prose works, except for the excellent condensation (about one-fifth of the original) of the *Journal*, as Tom Moore's Diary,) edited with an Introduction by J. B. Priestley, and published at Cambridge, England, by the Cambridge University Press, in 1925. (I have used these two editions in quoting from the biography of Byron and the *Journal*.) In 1964 the journal was reprinted in full by the Macmillan Company, and, also in 1964, the Oxford University Press brought out an edition of Moore's letters, edited by Wilfrid S. Dowden.

Most of Moore's books, in first or in other early editions, can be found in any large library. The following chronological list of first editions of his publications is largely indebted to one compiled by M. J. McManus that appeared in *The Dublin Magazine* in 1934, and was reprinted in *Thomas Moore*, by Seamus MacCall. I have omitted musical settings in which the words are merely incidental to the music; ascribed but nonexistent publications; and minor open letters or pamphlets.

Odes of Anacreon. London: John Stockdale, 1800.

Poetical Works of Thomas Little Esq., London: J. and T. Carpenter, 1801.

Epistles, Odes, and Other Poems. London: Carpenter, 1806.

Irish Melodies. Vols. 1 and 2. London: James Power; Dublin: William Power, 1808.

Corruption and *Intolerance.* London: Carpenter, 1808.

The Sceptic: A Philosophical Satire. London: Carpenter, 1809.

A Letter to the Roman Catholics of Dublin. London: Carpenter, 1810.

Irish Melodies. Vol. 3. London and Dublin: J. and W. Power, 1810.

Irish Melodies. Vol. 4. London and Dublin: J. and W. Power, 1811.

M. P., or The Blue-Stocking (selections). London: J. Power, 1811.

Intercepted Letters, or the Two-Penny Post-Bag (by "Thomas Brown the Younger"). London: J. Carr, 1813.

Irish Melodies. Vol. 5. London and Dublin: J. and W. Power, 1813.

Irish Melodies. Vol. 6. London and Dublin: J. and W. Power, 1815.

Sacred Songs. Vol. 1. London and Dublin: J. and W. Power, 1816.

Lalla Rookh, An Oriental Romance. London: Longman, Hurst, Orme and Browne, 1817.

Irish Melodies. Vol. 7. London: J. Power, 1818.

National Airs. Vol. 1. London and Dublin: J. and W. Power, 1818.

The Fudge Family in Paris (by "Thomas Brown the Younger"). London: Longmans, 1818.

The Works of Thomas Moore. Paris: Galignani et Cie, 1819.

National Airs. Vol. 2. London and Dublin: J. and W. Power, 1820.

Irish Melodies (first collection). Dublin: W. Power, 1820.

Same, corrected, with *Prefatory Letter on Music.* London: J. Power, 1821.

Irish Melodies. Vol. 8. London: J. Power, 1821.

National Airs. Vol. 3. London: J. Power, 1822.

National Airs. Vol. 4. London: J. Power, 1822.

The Loves of the Angels. London: Longmans, 1823.

Fables for the Holy Alliance (by "Thomas Brown the Younger"). Rhymes on the Road. London: Longmans, 1823.

Irish Melodies. Vol. 9. London: J. Power, 1824.

Sacred Songs. Vol. 2. London: J. Power, 1824.

Selected Bibliography

Memoirs of Captain Rock, the Celebrated Irish Chieftain, with Some Account of His Ancestors. London: Longmans, 1824.
Memoirs of the Life of the Right Honourable Richard Brinsley Sheridan. London: Longmans, 1825.
National Airs. Vol. 5. London: J. Power, 1826.
Evenings in Greece: (The First Evenings.) London: J. Power, 1826.
The Epicurean. A Tale. London: Longmans, 1827.
National Airs. Vol. 6: London: J. Power, 1827.
Odes upon Cash, Corn, Catholics, and Other Matters. London: Longmans, 1828.
Legendary Ballads. London: J. Power, 1828.
Letters and Journals of Lord Byron: with Notices of His Life. London: John Murray, 1830.
The Life and Death of Lord Edward Fitzgerald. London: Longmans, 1831.
The Summer Fête. London: J. Power, 1831.
Evenings in Greece: The Second Evening. London: J. Power, 1831.
Travels of an Irish Gentleman in Search of a Religion. London: Longmans, 1833.
Irish Melodies. Vol. 10. London: J. Power, 1834.
The Fudge Family in England. London: Longmans, 1835.
The History of Ireland. Vol. 1. London: published jointly by Longman, Rees, Brown, Green and Longman of Paternoster Row, and John Taylor, 1835.
The History of Ireland. Vol. 2. London: Longmans, and Taylor, 1837.
Alciphron: A Poem. London: John Macrone, 1839.
The History of Ireland. Vol. 3. London: Longmans and Taylor, 1840.
The Poetical Works of Thomas Moore, Collected by Himself. London: Longmans (10 vols.), 1841.
The History of Ireland. Vol. 4. London: Longmans and Taylor, 1846.
The Memoirs, Journal and Correspondence of Thomas Moore. Edited by Lord John Russell. London: Longmans (8 Vols.), 1853–56.
Prose and Verse, Humourous, Satirical and Sentimental, with Suppressed Passages from the Memoirs of Lord Byron, and Including Contributions to the Edinburgh Review between 1814 and 1834. London: Chatto & Windus, 1878. ("The "suppressed" passages are not suppressed; they were omitted by Moore as unneeded or irrelevant.)

SECONDARY SOURCES

Material useful to the student of Moore's writings may be found in the following biographical works; there are no pure critical works, but most of the biographies—and particularly those by Jones, Strong, and Gwynn—contain a large amount of critical analysis, both direct and quoted.

ENGLAND, DENZIL, *Thomas Moore. Contemporary Review*, MDCCC-XVIII (March, 1952) p. 157. An excellent short résumé of Moore's place in the literature of his time and ours; especially good on Moore's lighter poems.

GARNETT, RICHARD. *Essays of an Ex-Librarian.* New York: Dodd, Mead and Company, 1901. This originally appeared as the preface to a collection of "anecdotes" taken from Moore's *Journal,* published in London by Jerrold in 1899. Garnett is "dated" in his viewpoint, but as a man of letters himself he makes some shrewd appraisals of another litterateur.

GWYNN, STEPHEN L. *Thomas Moore.* London: The Macmillan Company, 1905. (One of the *English Men of Letters* series.) Short, but well-organized and fair.

HAZLITT, WILLIAM. *The Spirit of the Age.* London: Henry Colburn, 1825. (This may be found in Hazlitt's *Collected Works,* edited by A. R. Waller and Arnold Glover [London: J. M. Dent and Company, 1902], which I have used in quoting from Hazlitt.) The relevant article, "Mr. Thomas Moore and Mr. Leigh Hunt," gives a contemporary judgment of Moore's poetry by one of the best critics of his day. It is colored by Hazlitt's political disagreement with Moore, but not enough to disturb his balance.

JONES, HOWARD MUMFORD. *The Harp That Once.* New York: Henry Holt and Company, 1937. This is the best and fullest modern biography, though its emphasis is on Moore's life rather than on critical appraisal of his writing. However, as professor of English at Harvard and one of the most distinguished contemporary American literary critics, the author's evaluation of Moore's work and his place in English literature may be relied on for understanding and accuracy.

MAC CALL, SEAMUS. *Thomas Moore.* London: G. Duckworth & Co., Ltd., 1935. (One of the *Noted Irish Lives* series.) Inaccurate, but contains a useful bibliography of first editions of Moore's works.

MOORE, DORIS LANGLEY. *The Late Lord Byron.* Philadelphia: J. B. Lippincott Company, 1961. A detailed account of the controversy over the burning of Byron's Memoirs, including a complete statement of Moore's part in the affair. A portion of this book also appeared in *The Atlantic Monthly* in 1959.

SAINTSBURY, GEORGE. *Essays in English Literature.* London: Rivington, Percival and Company, 1896. A fair, sober estimate of Moore's

Selected Bibliography

work, written from the standpoint of the late nineteenth century.
STOCKLEY, WILLIAM F. P. *Essays in Irish Biography*. Cork: Cork University Press, 1933. An interesting slant on Moore from the rather prejudiced position of an ardent Irish patriot who was also a devout Roman Catholic.

STRONG, L. A. G. *The Minstrel Boy, A Portrait of Tom Moore*. New York: Alfred A. Knopf, 1937. (The original English edition appeared the year before.) A sympathetic work by a writer partly of Irish ancestry. Strong, who died in 1958, was well-known as a poet and novelist. He mentions in his book that Howard Mumford Jones was then preparing a "definitive" life of Moore. But Strong's biography (though also primarily concerned with Moore's personal life rather than with critical analysis) is, next to Jones's, the best modern work.

TUCKER, WYN J. *Literary Aspects of Ireland. Catholic World*, CXL (March, 1940), pp. 652–55. A brief but acute consideration of Moore, by the Professor of English in the University of Arizona.

Index

Index

Index